Persuasion

Unique Persuasion techniques for beginners. Complete guide how to use NLP and body language to understand human behaviors, mind games, brainwashing to protect yourself and those you love.

Author James D. Mill

Copyright © 2019 by James D. Mill

All rights reserved. No part of this publication may be reproduced, distributed, or transmitted in any form or by any means, including photocopying, recording, or other electronic or mechanical methods, without the prior written permission of the publisher, except in the case of brief quotations embodied in critical reviews and certain other noncommercial uses permitted by copyright law. For permission requests, write to the publisher at: permissions@ JamesDMill.com

Table of Contents

Introduction 1

Chapter 1   What Is Persuasion? 8

Chapter 2   Successful Persuasion Techniques 13

Chapter 3   The Power of Persuasion 30

Chapter 4   Persuasive Words 42

Chapter 5   How To Convince Someone Of Your Opinion 67

Chapter 6   How To Understand Body Language 76

Chapter 7   Brainwashing and Mind Games 92

Chapter 8   Neuro-Linguistic Programming 106

Chapter 9   Applied Persuasion 113

Chapter 10   Persuading and Influencing People Using Manipulation .. 122

Conclusion 140

Introduction

In our modern world, we rely the most on the use of persuasive tactics or techniques. Their strength depends on our ability to evaluate a situation and to choose the right weapons. Different psychologists have given different lists of basic tactics: these ones are offered to help you get a clear view in order to plan your influence strategy.

1. Persuade Only Those Who Can Be Persuaded

We can all be influenced at one time or another, provided the timing and the context is right. However, for some people, it can take a lot of persuading. Take a look at the politicians and their campaigns - they focus their money and their time almost exclusively on the small percentage of voters who are responsible for determining the outcome of an election. The very first step to successful persuasion is to identify and focus on the people who can, at that moment in time, be persuaded to follow you and your point of view. By doing this, a certain percentage of others - those who can't be persuaded at that moment in time - will be influenced later on to change their course.

2. Get Your Timing and Content Right

These are the building blocks of persuasion. Context is what provides a standard for what is and isn't acceptable. For example, an experiment carried out on Stanford prisoners showed that students who overachieve could easily be molded into prison guards with a dictatorial nature. The timing is what dictates what we are looking for from other people and from life. Often, when we marry, it is to someone very different to whom we may have been dating in our younger years, simply because what we want at any given time is subject to change.

3. Uninterested People Cannot Be Persuaded

You simply can't convince people to do something if they genuinely are not interested in what you have to say. In general, the human race is concerned primarily with their own individual selves and most of their time is spent thinking about three things – health, love, and money. The very first step to persuading someone is to learn to talk to that person about themselves. Appeal to their self-interest and you have their attention. Continue to do it, and you will hold their attention for long enough to persuade them.

4. Reciprocity is Compelling

Whether we like it or not, most of the time that someone does something for you, you feel innately compelled to return the favor. It's the way we are made, a survival instinct that goes back many millions of years. You can use that reciprocity to your advantage by giving someone something they want; you can then ask for something much more valuable back from them, and they will feel compelled to do it. The principle of reciprocation is more effective if you are the first one to give and if your gift is personal and unexpected.

5. Be Persistent but not Overbearing

If you are prepared to keep on asking for what you want, to continue demonstrating real value, you will ultimately succeed in the art of persuasion. Take a wander back through history and look at the vast numbers of figures who have persuaded people through persistence, in both message and endeavor. Look at Abraham Lincoln, look at what he lost – three sons, his mother, his girlfriend, one of his sisters. He failed abysmally in business, and he also lost at no less than 8 elections. Still, his persistence paid off when he was finally elected as President of the Unties States. He never gave up and neither should you.

6. Be Sincere in Your Compliments

Whether we admit it or not, compliments do have a positive effect on us, and we are much more likely to place our trust in a person who is sincere and who makes us feel good. Try it – be sincere when you compliment a person, pay them compliments for something that they honestly wouldn't expect it to. Compliment them on something they had to work for: it can be something as simple as their clothing choice. Don't compliment them on their beauty or on other things they were born with. It's quite easy once you learn how to do it, and it costs nothing. The rewards will speak for themselves.

7. Set Your Expectations

One of the biggest parts to persuasion is learning to manage the expectations of others when it comes to placing trust in you and your judgment. If a CEO were to promise his employees a pay increase of 20% and then give them 30%, he would be rewarded much more than the CEO who promised 20% and only delivered 10%. Learn to understand what other people expect of you and then over deliver on it.

8. Never Assume

This is a bad mistake to make: to assume what people are looking for. Instead, offer them your value. Take the sales world; often products and services are held back because it is assumed that people simply don't have the money to purchase them, or they have no interest in them. Be bold, get out there and say what you have to offer, say what you can do for them and leave the choice to them. Be persistent, and it will pay off.

9. Make Things Scarce

Virtually everything has a value these days, on a relative scale. We need the bare necessities to survive, so they have a far higher value than something we don't need. Often we want something because someone else has it. If you want to persuade people to want what you are offering, it may not be enough to point out the benefits of things or services we are offering. It could be much more effective if we would tell people about its uniqueness and what they could lose. That would create a scarcity feeling, and the less there is, the more people want it. The logic of scarcity is very simple: when something becomes scarce, people want it more.

10. Create a Sense of Urgency

One of the finer points of persuasion is being able to instill such a sense of urgency in people that they simply have to act straight away or miss out. If a person doesn't have any real motivation to want something now, they aren't likely to want it later on down the line either. It's down to you to persuade them that time is running out; persuade them now or lose them forever.

11. Images are Important

Most people respond better to something they can see. Quite simply if they can see it, then it's real; if you just talk about it, then it might not even exist. Images are potent, and pictures really do speak a thousand words. You don't actually have to use images, just learn how to paint that image in a person's mind.

12. Truth-Tell

Sometimes, hard though it may be, the easiest way to persuade a person to trust you is to tell them something that no one else will say, something about themselves. Facing up to the truth is often the most meaningful thing any of us will go through. Do it without any judgment and without an agenda, and you will be surprised at how quickly that person responds favorably to you.

13. Build Up a Rapport

The human race is a funny thing. We tend to like those who are more like us, and this often goes way beyond the conscious into the unconscious. By "copying" or matching your behaviors, regarding cadence, body language, patterns of language, etc. you will find that it is easier to build up a rapport with them and easier to persuade them to your way of thinking.

14. Be Flexible in Your Behavior

Have you considered why children are often so much more persuasive than adults are? It's because they are quite happy to work their way through a whole list of behaviors to get what they want – crying, being charming, pleading, trying to strike bargains, etc. Parent are stuck with just one response – No – which often turns to another – Yes. The more different behaviors you have in your repertoire, the more likely you are to be persuasive.

15. Be Detached and Calm

If you are in a situation where emotion is running high, you will always be the most persuasive person if you are calm, show little to no emotion and remain detached from the situation. In times of conflict, people will turn to you for help, and they will trust you to lead them in the right direction.

16. Use Anger in the Right Way

Most people really don't like conflict and if you are prepared to escalate a situation to a level of high tension and conflict, many of your adversaries will back down. Don't make a habit of doing this and never do it when you are in an emotional state or are on the verge of losing control. Do use anger in the right way to gain the advantage.

17. Be Confident, Be Certain

The most intoxicating and compelling quality is certainty. If you are confident and full of certainty, you will have the edge in persuading people to follow you. Believe in what you do, believe in what you say and you will always be able to persuade the next person to do what is right for them and to benefit you as well.

Chapter 1 What Is Persuasion?

"Thaw with her gentle persuasion is more powerful than Thor with his hammer. The one melts, the other breaks into pieces" - Henry David Thoreau

Historically, persuasion is rooted in ancient Greek's model of a prised politician and orator.

To make the list, a politician or orator needs to master the use of rhetoric and elocution in other to persuade the public. Rhetoric, according to Aristotle, is the "ability to make use of the available methods of persuasion" in order to win a court case or influence the public during important orations. On the other hand, elocution (a branch of rhetoric), is the art of speech delivery which may include proper diction, proper gestures, stance and dress. Although Grecian politics and orations seem clearly to be the genesis of persuasion, its use in the rapidly developing world of the twenty-first century goes beyond politics, oration and other human endeavors.

Persuasion, in the business domain, refers to a corporate system of influence aimed at changing another people, groups, or organizations' attitude, behavior or perception about an idea, object, goods, services or people. It often employs verbal communications (both written and spoken words), non-verbal communication (paralinguistic, chronemics, proxemics and so on), visual communication or a multimodal communication in order to convey, change or reinforce a piece of existing information or reasoning peculiar to the audience. Persuasion in business can come in different forms depending on the need of the management. For instance, business enterprise sometimes uses persuasion in cases like; public relations, broadcast, media relations, speech writing, social media, customer-client relations, employee communication, brand management and so on.

Persuasion, in psychological parlance, refers to the use of an obtainable understanding of the social, behavioral, or cognitive principles in psychology to influence the attitude, cognition, behavior or belief system of a person, group or organization. It is also seen as a process by which the attitude and behavior of a person are influenced without any form of coercion but through the simple means of communication. For instance, when a child begs his mother for candy and the mother refuses but instead proffers a better food for the child to eat while also encouraging him that it will make him grow bigger. The child gets excited and goes for the new alternative. In this way, the mother has been able to tap into his belief system without any form of duress. Hence, persuasion can also be used as a method of social control.

In the world of politics and governing today, persuasion still retains its role as one of the important means of influencing the behavior, feelings and commitment of the populace through the power of mass media. For instance, politicians sometimes use social media, television, radio, newspaper, magazine to persuade the populace to sponsor their political campaigns. Persuasion in modern politics is also observed through the use of authority in such situations where opponents of one political party influence on cross carpet to the other party with different promises in the form of power and immunity. In addition, the court still entertains the use of persuasion during the prosecution or defense of an accused.

Another way to see persuasion is through the intentional use of the means of communication as a tool of conviction to change attitudes regarding an issue by transferring messages in a free choice atmosphere. The verbal, non-verbal and visual forms of communication are manipulated just for the sole purpose of persuading an individual, group, or organization. Although communication is the most important and versatile form in which persuasion is manifested, it is worthy of note that not all forms of communication are intended to persuade. For instance, the celebration of a newly inaugurated president or governor circulated on the news cannot be classified as persuasion unless it is intended to impact something on the citizen of the country or react in certain ways.

We go further to look at other possible definition of persuasion in the circular world.

Persuasion is a concept of influence that attempts to change a person's attitudes, intentions, motivations, beliefs or behaviors. When a child begs his parent for candy and the parent says a big no to him, but the child insists on having candy even while knowing it might not be good for his health, persuasion is beginning to take place. Along the course of all of this, the parent will try to proffer a better food for the child to eat instead of the candy, the child gets excited and goes for the new alternative. In this way, the parent has won a banter of persuasion.

Persuasion on its own is a branch of communication and also popular as a method of social control, so it is worthy of note that not all forms of communication intend to be persuasive. Persuasion is also a process by which the attitude and behaviors of a person are influenced without any harsh treatments by simple means of communication from other people. Other factors can also determine a person's change in behavior or attitude, for example, verbal threats, a person's current psychological state, physical coercion etc.

Having discussed the meanings of persuasion, it can be observed that persuasion extends beyond a specific field as there are an intermingling of ideas from different areas of study. However, communication and psychology seem clearly to be in use in order for persuasion to take place. While communication provides the model as to how interlocutors in the art of persuasion get messages understood, psychology provides the model for the mental processes during persuasion.

Chapter 2 Successful Persuasion Techniques

"A heart can no more be forced to love than a stomach can be forced to digest food by persuasion" - Alfred Nobel

Firstly, I think it's a good idea to state exactly what persuasion is. It's simply the process or action taken by a person or group of people when they cause something to change. This will be in relation to another human being and something that changes their inner mental systems (attitudes, values & beliefs) or their external behavior patterns (actions & habits). The act of persuasion may also create something new within the person or may just modify something that already exists in their mind.

In my experience both types of persuasion have its own set of problems and obstacles, getting somebody to do something completely new can be challenging as they have no prior reference point for it and will naturally be cautious or even dubious about trying it. Similarly getting a person to change or modify an existing thought pattern or behavior can be equally as tough as they are already set in their ways. Remember humans are pattern seekers by nature and are looking to connect the dots and find evidence to back up what they already believe as it's easier than re-thinking the whole thing. It's your job to go along with these patterns of thought when you can but disrupt, break up and redirect them when you cannot (pointers on this to come).

In terms of the process, persuasion is usually comprised of three parts:

1. The communicator or source of persuasion
2. The actual persuasive nature of the appeal
3. The target person/audience of the appeal

All three elements need to be taken into account before attempting any high level persuasions. It's good practice to look around you in your daily life and watch out for when these subtle (and sometimes overt) persuasions are happening. It's good training for when you want to employ similar tactics yourself or just as importantly to make sure you are not on the end of something you do not want to be.

The 3 Aristotelian appeals

"Character may almost be called the most effective means of persuasion"

(Aristotle)

The ancient Greek philosopher Aristotle is perhaps the most famous arguer and persuader of all time. He believed that there were generally three ways a person could approach things when they indented to persuade and change the opinion of another person.

Ethos

The first of these appeals he described is Ethos, which focuses on attributes such as character, integrity and trust. It focuses on the reputation of a person, what they may have done in the past and what others speak about them today. Reputations can be a very important thing to protect especially for politicians in high office or anybody in the public eye who wants to maintain any degree of influence over others. It's OK to show character, that you are a human being just like everybody else and even have some flaws. The trick is to ensure that they are small enough or irrelevant enough for the target audience not to care too much about, but large enough to show you as a person of good values and virtues.

Lastly, Aristotle explains how credibility can play a large factor in someone's persuasive power. Much like Cialdini's modern principle of social proof, people will more likely believe something that is coming from a perceived expert in that field. So make sure you cultivate this impression where you can through strong affirmative communication and gestures.

Pathos

Pathos is a quality that is more concerned with evoking the emotions of the listener, seeking in some way to excite them or arouse interest in what you are saying. This can most effectively be done through storytelling and referencing situations where injustices may have occurred or innocent people adversely affected. In turn you may use Ethos to condemn such action and describe your own high values and beliefs about the matter.

Linguistics also plays a big role when it comes to the Pathos appeal as language is such an effective tool for eliciting emotional responses. A good speaker and orator will always plan their words carefully by using hot and cold keywords to either amplify (intentional, anger, fire) or subdue a situation (careful, smooth, irrelevant). The next time you are watching a politician in a parliamentary debate or taking questions from the press, watch how they inflate or downplay whatever they are referring to depending on the spin they want to put on it. It was my job to coach this into certain foreign leaders who weren't quite ready for release yet.

Logos

The final approach is Logos which is actually an appeal to logic, rational explanation and evidence towards the argument at hand. As well as being a philosopher, Aristotle was also a prominent scientist of his time and believed highly in the use of empirical evidence to prove a point. He tried to encourage this as much as possible within law making and common discourse alike. The courts were especially interesting to him as all three appeals could come into play. Pathos being evoked when somebody is trying to put a positive or negative spin on a statement, Ethos to establish a witness's credibility and finally Logos to provide the evidence.

So after reviewing some of the over arching persuasion principles, it's now time to delve into some of the specific strategies that you can apply in everyday discourse which also helped me carve out useful relationships in the field.

Persuasion is both an art and a science. It is a science because you must first learn the high level skills and principles required to persuade someone effectively. It is an art to know exactly when to employ the strategies for the best results. In a day, most of us find ourselves in many types of persuasive scenarios. So go over the following techniques and see how best you can apply them to your situation.

Start Small (Foot in the door)

The first principle is just like what it sounds, before asking anybody for any large favor or request, you initially ask for a smaller one first. By doing so, the person will develop a helpful mindset towards you. Once the small task is fulfilled, they will commit to fulfilling any larger task at some point in the future. It will also be easier for you to approach someone with a smaller task compared to asking for something bigger and more cumbersome, so that's where you should start.

Going about it systematically can help with getting the favor approved. This technique was tested out in 1966, when two Stanford professors divided 156 women into 4 groups. They asked the first 3 groups various simple questions about their kitchen. A week later, they asked the same women to catalog their kitchen products, no quick or easy task for these individuals. The first three groups showed a 52.8% success rate in cataloguing the products while the fourth group showed only a success rate of just 22.2%. This shows that asking for a smaller task before the bigger one can help increase chances of getting it done.

This is actually the main premise of a confidence trick that con artists often employ. They will initially ask for a small amount of money, a hundred dollars or so to bet on a certain stock on your behalf due to some "insider" knowledge. They will obviously return a win for the mark often doubling or tripling the initial stakes. They will then go back to the mark some weeks later to ask them to invest a little more, this time a few hundred dollars and turn around a similar result. This will escalate until enough trust is built within the relationship when the con artist will now offer the mark the big prize, the real inside bet that will make them millions. So the mark gladly hands over any winnings they've accumulated thus far and usually their entire savings to boot. However unsurprisingly they never usually see the con artist or their money ever again...

Anchoring

I touched on this within "Negotiation; An-Ex SPY's Guide". Anchoring refers to a technique where a person uses a benchmark to influence another person. This technique is widely used in many circumstances as it can be very efficient in garnering a positive result. Say for example you are trying to sell a ballpoint pen that is priced at $10. The customer negotiates it to $8. The customer will walk away happy knowing that a product's price was reduced to suit his or her need but in actuality, the price of the pen was increased just that morning from $6 to $10. So in effect, you manage to make a profit on the product and satisfy the customer at the same time, all by initially anchoring the price at a higher point to begin with.

This theory was tested by a group of economists who offered students 3 annual subscription selections to pick from when signing up for a popular magazine. The first option was to choose a web only version for just $59, the second was to choose the printed option for $125 and the third was to choose web and print for $125. 16 students ended up choosing the first option while 84 chose the third (nobody went for the second option). After a few days time, the second option was actually eliminated. It was interesting to note that the vast majority of the students who choose the third option stuck with it as the second option was a mere decoy placed to enhance the value of the third option. It worked as an anchor for students to compare with the third option.

Reversal Tagging

Reversal tagging is a simple and subtle sentence phrasing trick that can be used to gain compliance or agreement from somebody in general. It is a method that uses two opposing structures to a sentence, the first component being an affirmative statement and second being a tag question. The premise here is to make the initial statement to open the line of questioning but add the tag question to give the person a binary choice when answering. That way you can reframe whatever response they give to make it sound as if they are agreeing with you all along.

You might say to your spouse "You like this house, don't you?" They might reply "Yes, I like this place" to which your respond "As I thought, you like this place." However if you had gotten the opposite response i.e. "You like this house, don't you?" to which they replied "No, I don't like this place" you simply say "As I thought, you don't like this place."

Statements like this are designed to have a negative reversal element to them, such as "he did call you, didn't he?" If done correctly the structure of the statement should hide the command in the form of a rhetorical question, by first telling the person what they should be thinking but inserting the question that offers a level of disagreement but also implying that this is not wanted (as it would be contradictory towards the already made assertion).

The key to this working is ensuring that the first statement is a strong one as it will be the main persuasive component to the principle. "She's correct, isn't she?" is different from "She's not correct, is she?" These are both technically reversals but the first is much more affirmative and effective then the second. Also be careful not to take too long of a pause in between the two components of the statement or have a very obvious rising tone to the tag question "David's happy.... isn't he?" This may invoke confusion and suspicion or even contention of the point. So make sure it's it flows well and reasonably neutral in its intonation.

This technique can also be used when persuading a person to actually take action on something as opposed to simply agreeing with you. It's the same principle and structure but this time you state the negative first and take a longer pause before the tag question "You aren't able to do that.... are you?" If you imply to a person that they cannot do something it will evoke a reactive response to prove you wrong, you still add the reversal tag question to soften the statement. This is much like the principle of reverse psychology that I will explain in greater detail next.

Reverse Psychology

This one should be familiar with just about everyone as it is a common psychological tactic used when trying to get another person to take an action. However it can seem obvious and clichéd if not performed in the correct and subtle manner. It is essentially getting somebody to do something by initially suggesting that they do the opposite. It is also more effective if the suggestion evokes an emotional response as they are less likely to think it through rationally and just react. This is especially true when you are suggesting they cannot do something they are stating themselves (but you also want them to do) i.e. "I could finish this all today if wanted too" to which you reply "I'm sure you could, but you usually work to slowly..." They will more than likely do it to prove you wrong.

"Elegant persuasion is when the other person thought it was their idea"

(Marshall Sylver)

This principle is more likely to work with individuals who need to be in control more often than not, rebellious types like teenage children who naturally want to do the opposite to what their parents are telling them. It's actually termed "Reactance theory" and describes a scenario where a person feels like they have lost control and attempts to grab it back by doing the opposite of what they are asked, even if it is not in their best interest.

As I mentioned above, a reverse psychology statement needs to be done correctly to avoid detection as it is so common. Make sure you cloak the statement as much as possible and use a neutral or even dismissive tone to imply that you are indifferent to their response.

Cognitive Dissonance

You will know this feeling if you have ever noticed something "off" about a situation but you can't quite put your finger on it. As I've described in previous books, a spy's job is to notice baselines and norms in all situations so they know when something is amiss. When something isn't right it sets off a level of dissonance in the mind and subsequently triggers a response to act to make it right. People with OCD also know this feeling well as they might insist on having their desk arrangement a certain way for example, a pen pot or hole punch even a few inches out of place will cause a cognitive dissonance in their mind until the object is moved back to its original place. In fact cognitive dissonance is the process by which we naturally experience any real changes or differences in the world around us.

However the level of this dissonance also increases with the perceived importance of the situation, how far away the current position is compared to the original and lastly our perceived inability to rationalize the discrepancy away. For this reason, a cognitive dissonance conflict in our mind can be a very effective motivator for behavioral change. It is the most effective and productive way to release the tension and rectify the dissonance that exists. The other way would be to not change the behavior but instead justify it by changing the conflicting cognition or adding new ones to alleviate the old problem. In general terms this just means rationalizing the conflict away in your mind so it no longer affects you in the way it previously did.

Dissonance is also much more apparent when it comes to issues on self-image, nobody wants to feel stupid, immoral etc so a projection of one of these feelings can be a powerful trigger for behavior change. As a result, cogitative dissonance can play a very large and central role in the persuasion process or any attempt to change behaviors, values and beliefs. This dissonance tension can be applied in both acute bursts or over a longer sustained period of time. It works much like the reverse psychology principle I described above, and it is your job to find the cognitive norms in people's minds and disrupt them to a point where they want to make the behavioral change to fix it.

Counter-Attitudinal Advocacy

It is common place for people to state a view on something or support an opinion that they do not necessarily believe to be true themselves. This isn't as deceptive as it may sound as the things people do this with are often very small and well intended, like a white lie told to protect someone's feelings or where their own views maybe offensive in a situation. When this happens, we attempt to reduce the dissonance caused by justifying our actions as noble.

Now whether you believe this to be acceptable or that total and open honesty is the best course of action is irrelevant as you can use this natural human tendency to your advantage when persuading others. I have seen this happen within certain cults around the world and within gangs when changing people's beliefs to justify their behavior change in a more sinister way.

This persuasion principle like many others, actually ties in very closely with another which is "Incremental Escalating Requests." The idea is to offer the person very small rewards so that they do not attribute their behavior to any real change. But over time this effect escalates to a point where they are doing something radically different from where they started.

Try to do this in practice yourself, get people to go along with you on small points but on things that are directed towards the eventual persuasion goal. Make sure the points are small enough so that the internal justification for agreeing with you on them isn't significant enough for them to question or resist. After sometime, their beliefs should start to change to yours.

Perceived Self-Interest

As much as humans like to believe that they are generous and caring creatures, there is no getting away from the fact that we can ultimately be very self-serving as a species. Many experiments concerning game theory such as the "prisoner's dilemma" prove this time and again. Psychologists even argue that altruism is a self-serving act as by performing a task purely for another person's benefit (with seemingly no pay for ourselves) is actually only an attempt to garner the feel good factor we get from the empathy we receive as a result.

The idea on this one is simple, it is all about perception. If you can convince somebody to believe (whether it's true or not) that what they are doing is in their own best interest, then they are much more likely to go along with it. This is especially apparent when it comes to persuading or impressing people of higher stature than you, like your boss or employer. Say something like "I see my job as making you more successful" or "If I can make your life easier then I have done my job". This will endear a new or prospective employee to a boss greatly, as although you will gain some credit along the way, ultimately you do not want to steal the limelight too heavily from there person who pays your wages.

But as always, remember to do this in a genuine and tactful manner. You do not want to come across as being purely brown nosing as that will likely showcase your own WIIFM ("What's in it for me") thinking.

Disrupt-Then-Reframe (DTR)

This strategy is very similar to the "Offer Biasing" and "Russian Front" negotiation tactics I described within my book on the same subject. It's all about assessing norms once more and disrupting the way in which people think along those lines.

The idea is to put out a statement that is very far away from what the person's beliefs and ideals are to begin with. This is like offering them something they are very unlikely to want or accept. Then you follow this up with a much more rational request that the person will likely go along with as they are still making the comparison to the first one in their mind. This second suggestion will obviously be the one you are looking to persuade them towards.

It's a little like reverse tagging however it's performed in a slightly longer statement which you are also rephrasing and disrupting what you are saying. It can even be something nonsensical in nature as the aim is to just disrupt what is being said and being thought first and foremost.

Two researchers at the university of Arkansas Barbara Price and Eric Knowles put this theory to the test when they set up an experiment in which they would offer customers note cards by door to door sellers from some invented nonprofit organization for disabled children. The sellers would initially introduce themselves and their sales pitch before asking if the person would like to know the price of the cards. In some instances this disruption phrase was applied, in this case offering the cards "for 300 pennies" before stating, "that's just 3 dollars, it's a bargain!" The studies found that the DTR sales pitches were anywhere from 1.5-2 times more likely to convert when compared to the normal sales pitch.

This approach is based primarily on the studies of hypnotist Milton Erikson and his methods of deliberately disrupting peoples waking thought patterns and behaviors that would destabilize their habitual thinking and change it while the person was still somewhat unsure of what to think next. It's a kind of confusion tactic that allows you just enough time to reframe what the other person is thinking in a "hurt and rescue" type fashion.

This leads me onto the final persuasion tactic...

Hurt and Rescue principle

Again much like the "Russian Front" style negotiation tactic, the "Hurt and Rescue" principle is based off of evoking a level of fear or discomfort in the person initially. Then when they are assessing their options for other solutions, you offer them the one you are trying to persuade them towards. It's a way of manufacturing a level of discomfort before offering some form of relief from it.

Again like everything I'm suggesting in this book, be careful not to come across as intimidating or aggressive which can set off a 'fight or flight' response in the person that will be massively counterproductive here. This should in fact just be a subtle nudge in the right direction when done correctly.

You can say something like "I've noticed that you performance has dropped off recently to the point where we might have to cut your funding. Don't worry; I've convinced my seniors not to do that so long as you start meeting the metrics again."

Chapter 3 The Power of Persuasion

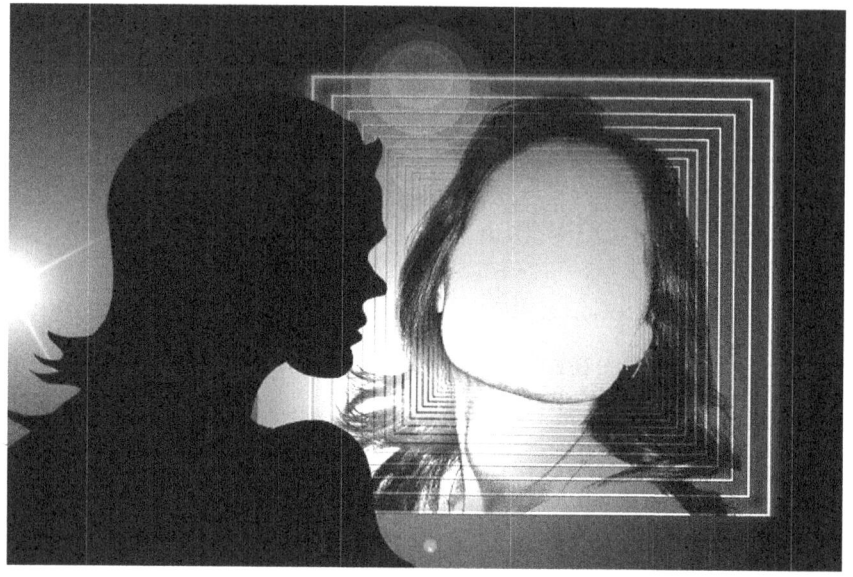

"Most people don't have the power of persuasion"
- James Altucher

When we lead another person to do something or make a certain decision of our own choosing, what is it that we are actually doing in order for this to happen? Are we actually sending out brainwaves or signals into the Universe that tell the other person what he or she will do? Of course, guiding another is possible with direct communication. You ask someone to do something and that person does it. Yes, this is a form of controlling someone, but it's with that person's willingness to carry out whatever it is that you have requested. You can even make someone else do a particular thing by using blackmail or threats. There is a multitude of possibilities when causing another person to perform something of your choosing which are both positive and negative. How about when you are able to do this and that person does not even know that it's being done?

The vast majority of everything that we do and every action that we take is a result of some form of conglomeration with others. This is excluding small decisions that we make daily and the routine tasks we do during our daily lives. Things as what to watch on television and when to turn that television on are not included in this topic. What is included are most of the major decisions that you, and everyone else, will make each day. These decisions are dealing with both work and outside of the workplace. We conglomerate more often than we realize. This is primarily because we, as human beings, are social creatures by our very nature. We tend to generally work together so that we all are satisfied and fulfilled.

Let's look at an example of how we allow our decision making to include others. The best example to use would be those who have families. This should include most everyone, but there are exceptions to every rule. When there are partners involved, most decisions made are done so with you working with your significant other. Deciding on a house to buy, without consulting your spouse about it, wouldn't go over too well. The same can be said with benign things such as what to make for dinner that night. The list of decisions can go on forever. Most of the time, your spouse probably is able to make his or her own decision without much guidance, but there may be times when you would like to help sway a particular decision in one way or another.

If you were about to purchase a new family car, and you wanted a certain color and model, but your wife didn't like the same, you would try to come up with reasons as to why she should change her mind and agree with you. This would be a form of direct communication, but you are still attempting to control her through a form of manipulation. You are already aware that she isn't agreeable with you on the specifications for the new car, but you are going to try to sway her anyway. You are trying to change her mind though, what is known as, persuasion. Persuading someone simply means that you are causing, by several methods, someone to do or believe something that they otherwise wouldn't. If you are able to convince your wife that the vehicle you like is better because it has all wheel drive, which is good for the winter, and she changes her mind because of this, you have persuaded her in that way.

Another way in which to look at the art of persuasion is what we do as parents. For those with children, you are most likely well acquainted with the ins and outs of persuasion. Parenting would be a horrible experience if we were to simply demand that our children do certain things. Imagine what kind of feedback you would get if you were to simply tell your child everything; he or she must do without ever giving any kind of explanation or reasoning behind your thought processes. You wouldn't do this long before you were met with a great amount of resistance. Therefore, parents need to develop a means of persuasion which best suits our particular child based on his or her characteristics and understanding.

What about decisions made by those who are not in large families or that have children? Excluding the workplace, would there be times in which that person's decisions were due to the opinions and ideas of others? How about what that person wears each day? Even if you are not in a relationship and you have no children, there are still considerations in which partially lie with others. When you go to the store to buy clothes for work, what factors come to play with your purchase? Of course, things such as comfort and price are factors. What about style? A man isn't going to buy a lady's shirt and wear it to work. That isn't because it's more expensive or less comfortable. It's probably because he does not want others to see him wearing ladies clothing while working. With this, he has allowed the thoughts and opinion of others to dictate, in some fashion, what he will wear to work.

In the previous examples and scenarios, each person is aware of what is going on. The wife who does not like the all-wheel-drive car knows that her husband does like it. She is aware that he is trying to cause her to change her mind about the purchase. Even being aware of this, she is receptive to his attempt at persuading her and he ends up being successful. The kid knows that the parent is trying to lead him to make a specific decision that he may have initially been against, but he knows that his parent believes it to be in his best interest. The clothes that the gentleman purchased at work were purchased by those standards which have been set by society in general.

Now, let's look at persuasion in the workplace. It's here where your ability for persuasion and to manipulate has the best chance of paying off in a positive way. Why do we go to work in the first place? In order to best know how to use manipulation at work, it's a good idea to understand why it is that people go to work. There are only a few possible reasons. First, and most common, people work in order to get paid. Everyone needs money to live. Most believe that the more money, the better. Therefore, many workers will gladly come to decisions they believe will increase their pay or advance their career. Another reason for working is to actually provide a service to others or provide some sort of goods. However, going back to the basics, it all leads to the dollar. Keep this in mind.

In the workplace, when is there a need for persuasion or even manipulation to begin with? A good guess would be if someone at work wants to manipulate another, it's likely because such decision or action will benefit him by advancement or by more money. If you are interested in learning how to manipulate or how to persuade while at work, why do you want this? I'm sure it's for advancement or a raise. Remember, everyone at work is there for the same reasons. If you want to manipulate a coworker, find a way to make that person believe that he or she will also benefit from whatever it is that you want. They are there for the same reason as you. Use that knowledge to your advantage.

The other side to this is somewhere I wouldn't recommend going, but it's worth mentioning. The best method is to identify what the other person wants and make them believe that to be a result. Likewise, you could also identify things the other person fears. This is totally within the scope of manipulation and not with persuasion. If someone isn't given a good reason or something to gain from an action, that person may fall to the thought of losing something valuable. This happens with bad management often. Threaten to take someone's job and they will do a lot for you.

Here is something to remember. If you manipulate someone by using negative tactics, you have forever destroyed any possibility of a positive relationship with that person. You will be an enemy. Yes, you may be feared and through this gain some control over that person but the outcome will always be negative. If you choose to carry out your plan using positive tactics, you not only can have the same outcome but can also gain other things for future use. Things such as having a friend in certain positions can go a long way. This is where the patience, mindfulness, and sight of the big picture come into play.

Another fact that needs to be remembered is that we don't cause any other person to do anything at all. We are each responsible for our own decisions and, at the end of the day, we are the ones making those choices. No matter how skilled someone may be at manipulation, that person will never actually make another person's decision for them. The best we, as manipulators, can do is lead those people to their decisions. Remember this key point also. In order to manipulate anyone, you must make that person believe they need what they are choosing and it's that person who is making the decision. This is the most important part of learning to manipulate others.

The last key factor, which is especially relevant in the workplace, is there is a difference between manipulation and persuasion. The two different terms are commonly used interchangeably but are different. A manipulator tends to be more aggressive and requires less of the person in which he or she is trying to control. Also, when it comes to negative or malicious intent, manipulation is much more common than techniques of persuasion. Manipulation will often include things such as threats and blackmail. Results from this are commonly negative and harm is usually caused. Persuasion is more of a fluid, give and take, technique and usually has better outcomes. Those who use persuasion count on participation, and common knowledge of what's happening, from those who are the target. This is much like a teacher and student relationship. The defining difference between persuasion and manipulation is simply whether or not the person doing it intends for the result to be best for all involved.

Just like with every other ability that isn't possessed by everyone, there are principles associated with persuasion. Principality is very important and parallels with character. A lack of principles leads to someone who is trifling and harmful to others. Let's look at some of these and how they apply. The first, and most basic, principle has already been mentioned in this chapter. Its persuasion is not manipulation. It's important to remember this because there is a big difference between the two and most people want no part of manipulation. This is referring to those practicing it and not the victims. Another principal will be mentioned again several times throughout this book. That is persuading the persuadable. This means you need to select your subject, person to persuade, correctly and make sure the timing is correct as well. Context is important as well. Now, keep this in mind. For someone to be persuaded, he or she needs to be interested. If they are not interested, there isn't going to be a way of persuading them. Think of a child in school who does not pay attention. That child isn't retaining any of the information from class. The teacher is attempting, or should be attempting, to pass on information to the student but, because of disinterest, that student isn't learning.

There is a principle that states, "reciprocity compels." Humans inherently want to return favors. This is where reciprocity comes into play. This will be further discussed later in this book, but payback is a great tool for persuasion and even manipulation. Another is persistence pays. This should be good common sense. I once heard a story of a fish that was in a fisherman's bucket. The fish kept leaping out of the bucket and onto the ground. After doing this several times, the fisherman finally put that fish back into the pond. Another principle is to be sincere when complimenting and never lie. Don't assume anything either. Always try to build a rapport with the other person. This will prove extremely beneficial. It's almost impossible to persuade someone at all without some kind of rapport. It's possible to manipulate but not persuade.

Some other principles are to create scarcity. "Hurry and come because there are only a few left in supply!" This is something you will see on television commercials for automobiles. Along with this, set expectations this is dealing with others and not yourself. You need to understand their reasoning behind their expectations. There is a need for behavioral flexibility and the transfer of energy. You need to motivate and excite others and not drain them of all their energy. Not go too far and become spastic. Be sure to clearly communicate and learn to properly articulate your words. This gives the appearance of intelligence, professionalism, and know-how. Along with this, learn to be confident and never appear timid or to be second-guessing you.

Now, let's look at the primary skills one need possess in order to become a master manipulator or someone of great persuasion. Each requires a skill set which is unique. Both require a good deal of intelligence. If you are not intelligent enough to understand your target and circumstances, you may as well hang it up. Mindfulness, or the knowledge of your surroundings, is key to success. Another form of needed intelligence is what is known as, emotional intelligence. The person of persuasion needs to be skilled with this type of intelligence.

Assertiveness is also a good trait to possess. Those who tend to be shy or non-controversial are not usually good at guiding others. If you have a hard time leading yourself, you can't lead others. This is just good common sense. In addition, there is also a need for patience and the ability to stand back and just watch. Impatient people are not good at persuasion or manipulation. This is due to the process, more often than not, requiring some time and attention. Unless you are planning on taking a firearm and pointing it at the person you want to do something, then telling them what to do, you will need some time to get it done. Remember, you are not making the decision. The other person makes it and you are just trying to lead that person there.

Charisma is important too. You need to come off as a likable person. We tend to go along with and agree with those whom we like. Take politicians for example. One of the first characteristics a politician tries to portray is likeability. "I'm a nice guy. Yes, I'm trustworthy and hardworking, but I'm really nice. Vote for me because you will like me." That probably sounds like a familiar statement does not it? That politician is beginning the task of persuasion. He or she is trying to make you decide to vote for him or her.

The few traits mentioned, are the basic building blocks with the techniques of manipulation and persuasion. As with all other rules, there are exceptions, but more often than not, a good manipulator needs to be intelligent, charismatic, and assertive. Then he or she needs to combine all three and then apply them with diligence and patience. A manipulator must know his or her subject well in order to really manipulate. Again, that person is actually making his or her own decision. You, as the manipulator, must make that person think that it's in his or her best interest. This is unless you are going to use trifling techniques, such as blackmail, but then you don't really need the first three traits anyway. A person who blackmails need only have one thing. That is what information, or ammunition, he or she plans on using. This takes no skill. It only takes the ability to not care about others.

In order to really lead a person to some decision, you must look at all aspects of the situation. First, be sure that you know what it is that you want from the situation. Be sure of it. Then you need to find a few positives for the other person too. You need to make your target feel like you are not leading him or her on in any way. Make them feel like they are in control and are making the decision alone without your intervention. This is the best method because it allows for no ill-will to develop and all bridges will remain intact. Also, some people resent others leading them to make decisions, also known as persuasion, and they will be less likely to go with the program. So, make them think they are wearing the "big boy" pants.

Before you really begin to work toward your goal of persuasion, make sure that you have everything lined up. You have thought of many possible scenarios and setbacks along with how to handle them. Don't start with having only one or two benefits to lead your target into believing they are going to receive. Think of as many as possible. Also, think of negatives that are likely if they don't come to a certain decision you are planning. You make them see it like this; to make the decision leads to the land of milk and honey and to not make that decision can be threatening in some way. This isn't blackmail and don't take it to a dark place. Tread lightly with this and tailor it according to the situation and those involved.

Chapter 4 Persuasive Words

"You can change your world by changing your words... Remember, death and life are in the power of the tongue" - *Joel Osteen*

I'm sure that right now you're aware of the fact that words aren't just strings of letters sewn together with ink. They have a hidden power waiting for you to unleash. Words are cues; words are triggers. You can use them unconsciously, just like 99 percent of people do, or you can use them correctly and completely take advantage of their power. It's your choice. You have the ability to transform a bored "Eh, whatever..." into an enthusiastic "Wow, that's it!"—don't waste it.

Words can make you go from laughing your ass off hard to fuming with fury; they can take you from a skeptical "Nah..." to an uncontrollable urge to decide "Now!". How so? Well, I can answer you with just one word: emotions.

In fact, there are highly emotional words that can transform an absolute no into an almost yes and a "Maybe..." into "For sure!". They've been used in every kind of advertisement and marketing for ages, and I'm sure you've seen them time and time again. If they work so well, why don't you use them? It's time to switch on your awareness and exploit their power to improve your social and dating life, your communication skills, your career, your sales...and pretty much every other area of your life.

As you may know, people's actions are driven by specific underlying emotions—if you can control the latter, you'll have control over the former. For example, when you're trying to get someone to agree with you, what you are really doing is trying to induce empathy so that they can see and accept your point of view.

So...what are these words? Well, I've created a long list and you'll find it in the next pages. Keep in mind that they are proven to evoke certain emotions every time—both negative and positive. This last distinction doesn't really matter; what is most important is your ability to evoke strong emotions that drive your prospects to take immediate action. And if you'll start implementing these words in your online and offline communications, that's exactly the result you'll get.

Before jumping into the list with you, I want to share here a 3-step plan to make the most out of these words:

First step: Identify the desired action you want your prospects to take (for instance: like, share, comment, buy, subscribe...).

Second step: Determine the exact emotional state that will drive that specific action (for instance: inspired, relaxed, confused, fearful, curious...).

Third step: Pick a bunch of words from the list and sprinkle them throughout your content.

Emotional State: Curiosity

Curiosity is a necessary state of mind for you to instill in your prospects and readers if you want to hook them quickly. These words are particularly useful in headlines, titles, and whenever you want your prospect to be gripped by an unwavering desire to click, read, and learn more.

Controversial

Secret

Confidential

Forbidden

Banned

Underground

What no one tells you

Have you heard

Cover-up

Behind the scenes

Secret agenda

Censored

Secret plot

Insider

Concealed

Off the record

Confessions

Unbelievable

Covert

No one talks about

Insider's scoop

Blacklisted

Intel

Hidden

Underground

Emotional State: Urgency

As you now, the feeling of urgency is often necessary to get a prospect to decide fast, right in the moment. This is one of the most powerful agents of influence, so be sure to take advantage of it inside your content and all kinds of communications. From setting up a date with a girl via text to selling a high-ticket product, make sure to sprinkle these words in your conversations to put some pressure on the other person—and, ultimately, to get to a yes quickly.

Missing out

Left behind

Magical

Instantly

Magnificent

Miracle

Most important

Profitable

Startling

Strongly agree

Revolutionary

Safe

Proven

Quick

Results

Save

Sensational

Should

Strongly recommend

Worthwhile

Deadline

Strongly suggest

Superb

Remarkable

Superior

Tremendous

Truly

Seize

Bargain

Trustworthy

Extra

Fortune

Discount

Explode

Freebie

Reduced

Instant savings

Skyrocket

Immediately

Urge

Limited

Imminently

Jackpot

Emotional State: Confusion and Helplessness

Confusing your prospect is not something to avoid every time—it may be useful in the right moment. These words are especially helpful when you want your prospect to question the status quo, accept the challenge to escape his or her comfort zone, feel some FOMO, or respond to an "us vs. them" frame inside your content.

Indecisive

Doubtful

Uncertain

Hesitant

Disillusioned

Perplexed

Embarrassed

Distrustful

Stressed

Uncomfortable

Dishonest

Disdainful

Misgiving

Unsure

Tense

Manipulative

Authoritative

Condescending

Judgmental

Argumentative

Distracted

Off-kilter

Frenzied

Disoriented

Blushing

Fatigued

Inferior

Awkward

Incapable

Distressed

Pathetic

Woozy

Distraught

Overwhelmed

Paralyzed

Vulnerable

Incompetent

Trapped

Squirming

Incapacitated

Jittery

Twitching

Compulsive

Uncaring

Suspicious

Anxious

Uninterested

Unresponsive

Terrified

Alarmed

Panicked

Deceived

Helplessness

Threatened

Cowardly

Insecure

Disempowered

Doomed

Emotional State: Anger

Even though anger is a powerful emotion, you should not be afraid of it. Instead, you can use it to your own advantage during a sale or any kind of interaction. Anger is a high-arousal, physiological, emotional state that can help drive immediate actions, such as getting support for a cause or sharing content because of the utter outrage felt.

Provoke

Ordeal

Severe

Shameful

Outrageousness

Repulsive

Scandal

Corrupting

Damaging

Deplorable

Shocking

Terrible

Wicked

Aggravate

Tragic

Unreliable

Disastrous

Unstable

Agony

Appalled

Atrocious

Disadvantages

Enraged

Offensive

Disgusted

Ticked off

Revengeful

Dreadful

Eliminate

Harmful

Harsh

Inconsiderate

Resentful

Malicious

Aggressive

Frustrated

Controlling

Infuriated

Critical

Violent

Sadistic

Spiteful

Vindictive

Furious

Agitated

Antagonistic

Repulsed

Rebellious

Exasperated

Quarrelsome

Venomous

Impatient

Contrary

Scornful

Self-hating

Desperate

Alienated

Pessimistic

Sarcastic

Poisonous

Jealous

Retaliating

Reprimanding

Powerless

Despicable

Unjustified

Condemning

Violated

Dejected

Vilified

Emotional State: Safe and Satisfied

Great for sales pages when you want to evoke a feeling of safety in your audience's choice. As you know, safety is a very important fundamental in communication—not only in sales, but also in every kind of interaction. You should always make the other person feel safe and secure in the first place, so that you can easily build a relationship of trust and transparency.

Accurate

Honest

Truthful

Guaranteed

Highly effective

Instantly

Advantage

Introducing

Freedom

First ever

Investment

Always

A cut above

Bargain

Certain

Certainly

Easy

Confident

Ecstatic

Effective

Convenient

Definitely

Highly likely

Delighted

Emphasize

Extremely

Conscientious

Authentic

Approving

Honored

Privileged

Adaptable

Relaxed

Astonishing

Genuine

Astounded

Self-sufficient

Assured

Fulfilled

Reliable

Sure

Excellent

Solid

Responsible

Trusting

Stable

Supportive

Absolutely

Clarity

Transparency

Secure

Humility

Bargain

Emotional State: Happy and Alive

These are great words to use when you're selling health-based products or services, or anytime you want your prospect to be in a highly positive, vibrant, and energetic mood. By boosting his emotional state during the sale process, he'll be more inclined to buy from you; but even if he doesn't, he will at least associate those positive feelings with you, and he may buy from you in the future.

Blissful

Delighted

Joyous

Overjoyed

Innocent

Child-like

Gleeful

Thankful

Festive

Satisfied

Cheerful

Ecstatic

Jovial

Sunny

Elated

Lighthearted

Jubilant

Fun-loving

Glorious

On top of the world

Playful

Gratified

Euphoric

Courageous

Energetic

Frisky

Youthful

Vigorous

Animated

Spirited

Liberated

Optimistic

Thrilled

Wonderful

Intelligent

Exhilarated

Funny

Spunky

Tickled

Glowing

Creative

Bright

Encouraged

Blessed

Vibrant

Constructive

Helpful

Resourceful

Comfortable

Pleased

Surprised

Serene

Bountiful

Emotional State: Inspired

An important part of selling and building a positive relationship in general is inspiration. By using the following words, you can motivate and inspire the people around you, making them feel like they are capable and in control of their lives…even though you may secretly be the one behind their actions and behavior.

Motivated

Eager

Keen

Earnest

Inspired

Enthusiastic

Bold

Brave

Daring

Hopeful

Upbeat

Assured

Clear

Balanced

Fine

Okay

Grateful

Carefree

Adequate

Fulfilled

Genuine

Authentic

Forgiving

Sincere

Uplifted

Unburdened

Confident

Self-sufficient

Reliable

Sure

Unique

Dynamic

Tenacious

Cooperative

Productive

Exuberant

In the zone

Responsive

Conscientious

Approving

Honored

Privileged

Adaptable

Empowered

Focused

Capable

Emotional State: Relaxed and Peaceful

These words are perfect in case you're selling products or services that offer mental peace and relaxation. They can evoke this exact mood, which is going to put the prospect into a trance-like state, and this means more and easier sales for you.

At ease

Calm

Comfortable

Relaxed

Carefree

Quiet

Grateful

Serene

Certain

Bright

Blessed

Forgiving

Balanced

Fulfilled

Genuine

Authentic

Sincere

Self-sufficient

Confident

Glowing

Radiant

Reflective

Grounded

Beaming

Smiling

Unhurried

Open-minded

Unassuming

Trusting

Efficient

Non-controlling

Supported

Fluid

Light

Rested

Spontaneous

Aware

Healthy

Graceful

Natural

Meditative

Still

Waiting

Laughing

Steady

Centered

Clear

Stoic

Placid

Aligned

Chapter 5 How To Convince Someone Of Your Opinion

"Life is always going to be stranger than fiction, because fiction has to be convincing, and life doesn't " - Neil Gaiman

When you find yourself needing to convince someone of your opinion, you are already in a conflict situation. Most people would rather do anything but be found conflicting. They would rather bite their tongues even when they know they are right, rather than put forward conflicting ideas and have to waste their strength arguing about it. It takes courage to speak up because it demonstrates your insight and your value to a team. If you choose not to speak up, you risk being branded as ineffective and redundant, and this could be the end of your career, friendship, marriage, and other social associations.

Most of us fear to express our opinions because we perceive that it will lead to an engaging tedious battle of opinion. The reality is that persuasion is all about telling someone what he wants to hear to be convinced. When you want to persuade, do not begin by blatantly expressing your controversial opinion, start by first considering what your audience wants, taking yourself out of the equation, and focus on connecting with your audience on the topic.

How To Persuade

Whenever you have a valid point of disagreement, nothing should keep you from expressing your opinion. However, if you need to be heard, go about it with some form of decorum so that you know what to say, how to say it, and when to say it. Here are a few guidelines to help you through it:

1. Choose Your Battles

If you walked a mile asking the people you met to give their opinions and views about a particular topic, the chances are that you would find quite a number who would disagree with you. The issues could range from trivial matters such as how to press the toothpaste tube to serious matters like disciplining kids. In almost all issues of life, expect some opposition. People will not always agree with you, and you do not have to conflict with them every time.

You cannot afford to go fighting or to argue with people everywhere. That would wreck your social life and even deny your inner peace. Instead, choose to ignore the trivial issues and only focus on the things that matter. When you do this, even those around you will respect you. You have very limited social capital- how much of it are you willing to risk on conflicts because you insist on speaking your mind all the time?

Always think before you engage with others, and weigh the situation to see whether the issue at hand is worth your attention. Most of the time, it does not.

2. Give It Some Thought

When you have thought about the issue and felt that you need to speak up, be silent and rethink your position. Are you sure that you want to take that position on the matter? Is that the right thing to do? Are there any supporting facts?

Having these thoughts will keep you from jumping on to a topic with minimal information and embarrassing yourself. Giving your ideas a second thought will also ensure that you have all the facts straight, and where needed, you may even change your mind. You could also realize that the issue in question is not worth your time, and you may give up on the issue entirely.

3. Avoid Being So Emotional

It is risky to get into an argument or confrontation when you are overly anxious, angry or resentful; doing it will get you spewing venom you would regret. Your counterparts will also be provoked to become harsh and unreasonable, and in the end, you will have prompted the situation to escalate to a massive issue while it could have been resolved rationally.

If you want to get the respect of your peers, your seniors and your juniors, stick to reason and only engage a reasonable amount of emotion in your undertakings. If you are always reactive to situations and handle your issues led by emotions, you will appear irresponsible, and people will not want to be around you.

If a situation aggravates or excites you too much, take a step back, take some deep breaths, relax and stay calm so that you can address people respectfully.

4. Ensure That You Are Not Making Things Worse

Sometimes you want to find a solution to a problem by putting your views across, but you end up making things worse. It happens to us all. However, the frequency of this happening will lower if you purpose to engage only in conversations and arguments that will lead to something productive. Stay away from idle talk that is meant to bring people down.

5. Do Not Insist on Your Way All the Time

Some people go by the erroneous 'my way or the highway' philosophy. Thinking that you are always right, but others are wrong is a sign of pride. Only a person who is so full of himself, a narcissist, will think that he is always right and cannot make mistakes.

Instead, you should pass your views as opinions to be considered rather than as the final decisions. Doing this will more likely produce a favorable response from your audience compared to imposing your will on them. The moment you force the other party to take a defensive position, know that you blew it already.

6. Let the Facts Lead

Your opinion is an opinion like that of any other individual, and it is based on your intuition and the information you have so far. Others around you could also have influenced your stand on any particular issue. For these reasons, opinions are quite subjective. Therefore, while you need to speak confidently about what you think, ensure that you stick to the merits of your position, and back them up with data and statistics.

7. Allow the Other Side A Chance

Your opinion, even when it is right, does not have to carry the day. There could be bits about the other side's view that could build on your ideas. Therefore, as you argue out your point, come up with creative ways to incorporate the other party's opinions too. Give support to their ideas and way of reasoning, and you will see that they will start to be friendlier and accommodating of your opinions too.

Methods Of Persuasion

Below is a brief discussion of methods you can use to persuade someone to take up your ideas:

1. Questions

The questioning method is used to grasp the attention of your audience. When asked a question in a discussion, people begin to think about the appropriate answer to the question, and they also wonder the reason you asked them that particular question. However, you ought to be careful and to only ask questions that will add to your discussion because undoubtedly, your audience's minds will waver as they think of the right response to give. To get the right results, ensure that the questions you ask are short, simple, and logical. Let the questions inspire deeper thinking rather than taking away the audience's attention from your discussion.

2. Repetition

Repetition serves to incite and improve your brain's retention power. Once something is repeated to you, the odds of it getting stuck to your memory increase. Ensure that the sentences you speak highlight the keywords you want your audience to remember, and make an effort to repeat the most significant sentences or words. Place them strategically, and where possible, have your audience repeat them out loud, or put them down on paper.

3. Use Simulations

This is an excellent method for convincing strangers because you have not related before, and you cannot say anything about their mental abilities. You cannot also predict how they will react to certain statements, especially when discussing controversial issues. Using simulations creates an analogy by taking out the names of real places, people, and other things that could distract the listener and take his mind away from the subject.

For example, if you want to convince a college dropout to return to school, avoid mentioning places and names that could change the course of your discussion and shift it in an unfavorable direction. Do not mention the names of people that dropped out of school and succeeded like Bill Gates or Mark Zuckerberg. Do not also mention the names of people that dropped out of college and failed. Your aim should be to convince your audience, based on the unique circumstances that getting back in college would be the best decision he can make.

When you stick to the student's unique circumstances, he is likely to reflect on the reasons you gave and find some inspiration to finish his education. Giving examples of what other people did does not help much, what would help him is drawing the inspiration from within when times get difficult, rather from other people's stories. Sure, mentorship is a useful motivator, but the spirit in a man is what keeps him pushing and motivated, not the experiences of others.

4. Refute the Opinions of Others

Refuting can be difficult for many people, especially for those who hate or fear confrontations. It is also challenging because it requires a person to pay close attention to the opinions the other person has expressed, break it into smaller ideas, and then go about disapproving every one of them. Once you have knocked all of them down, now present your opinion and show how it is the better opinion. It is crucial that you rely on logic and reason throughout this process and present compelling facts that the other person knows about. That way, the other person will see the logic in your ideas and take them up.

As you present your ideas, the most important thing to do is to ensure that you have proof of your opinions. Of course, some beliefs cannot be proven, such as the question of taste (you cannot say you are right for finding an ice cream flavor sweeter than the other), because neither opinion could be wrong. However, in matters where you can provide proof, be sure to provide it.

Facts give the illusion that what you are saying is accurate and irrefutable. Therefore, when trying to convince people to take up your opinion, persuade them that it is a fact, even when it is not. Sadly, sometimes people twist the facts, but this is not something you should be engaging in.

Manipulators convince you that their opinions are better than yours by first getting into your head to see what you already know. Many of them will get you talking, and as you go on and on, they will be collecting information, wanting to see just how much you know.

From there, the manipulator cleverly repeats the facts you just stated back to you, adding in some more details. You will think that you are adding to your knowledge, but the truth is that these facts may not even be real. The manipulator might be making them up or twisting information to favor them. You see, there are very many ways to manipulate information. Some people, instead of agreeing with what you know, will go the other way and begin to discrediting what you know by presenting it as faulty. They do this by bending the facts a bit or presenting new crafted facts to the table. You end up denying the truth you already knew and taking up erroneous information. By the time you realize it, the person will have gotten away with much.

Chapter 6 How To Understand Body Language

"I don't think people are going to talk in the future. They're going to communicate through eye contact, body language, emojis, signs" - Kanye West

Body language is crucial to understanding other people, which means it is crucial if you want to be able to influence other people. When you understand body language, not only will you be able to watch the other person and understand his or her thought processes in real time, but you will also be able to tweak your own body language in ways that may make the other person relax or be more willing to speak with you. You can also understand the intent of others when you keep an eye on their body language. You will be able to tell more-or-less what mood they are in just at a glance if you can understand how to read them.

You can develop rapport through body language, meaning you will develop some sort of perceived closeness, if you know what you are doing. If you have more rapport with someone, you are more likely to get him or her to agree to do something for you if and when you may need it. This chapter will guide you, body part by body part, in what different types of body language mean. The next time you go out or are with a group of people, try reading the other people through looking for the several signs listed in this chapter — you might be surprised to find that you can influence the dynamics of the group by taking on some of the language as well.

Arms

Arms, in general, are quite dexterous — they are easy to move in a wide range of ways due to the abilities of the joints and the general movements. Arms can move up, down, sideways, outward, inward. They can be lifted and hunched. Arms are also fantastic measures of the other person's mental state. They are quite expressive, and while people will generally try to control their arms to hide their body language, there are ways to catch it in action.

Arms held back

When arms and shoulders are held back, they are general out of reach and harder to grab during a potential physical attack. This is a sign of defensiveness or discomfort.

Arms reaching forward

When you reach your arms out, you are doing one of two things, and context determines which of the two are being done. Either you are reaching out in comfort of someone else, or you are reaching out aggressively. Typically, it is seen as an attack when it is done quickly or with any other aggressive signs, and likewise, it may be seen as a sign of comfort to someone close to you when done gently and slowly.

Crossing arms

This is essentially creating a barrier. It conveys defensiveness, shyness, discomfort, a lack of confidence, or mistrust. This is physically protecting the vital organs within the chest, creating one more barrier between yourself and whoever you are currently interacting with. It also occurs when someone has just heard bad news — when the crossed arms are paired with gripping the arms with hands as well, it is typically an attempt to self-soothe.

Expanded arms

When you expand your arms and shoulders, opening up your chest, you are showing signs of confidence. This makes you seem larger and more confident and comfortable in your surroundings, whereas withdrawing your arms and shoulders implies defensiveness or discomfort.

Raised arms

Arms raised upward into the air are typically some sort of punctuation of whatever emotion is being felt — think of this as the exclamation point of emotions. If the person is happy and raises his arms, he is likely ecstatic. If she is angry and does so, she is probably furiously frustrated. If afraid, he may be absolutely terrified as he runs away.

Still arms

When arms are held still, either completely flat at their sides, or when using one arm to hold onto the other, it implies that the other person is lying or being deceitful somehow. This behavior is the other person's attempt at controlling his body language in an attempt to hide something.

Body

Paying attention to the body's general demeanor and proximity is also incredibly important when attempting to read someone. You can tell how interested or open someone is based on natural distance kept, or even how closely they seem to mimic you. When you are able to understand this, you are able to tailor your own actions to get the reactions you want.

Mirroring

Mirroring refers to the unconscious tendency to mimic what someone you are close to is doing in the moment. You may repeat their body language back, crossing your legs when the other person does, or taking a drink at the same time. This is done to people with whom you are close, or that you like. You are likely to mirror someone that you feel comfortable with in the moment, or you are interested in. This is a good thing — if you notice that the other person is mimicking you, you have a pretty good indication that the other person is comfortable with you or likes you. In an interview, this is a good sign thing are going well, and if a client is doing so, the client probably really trusts you. If you notice that the other person is not mirroring you, you can begin to mirror the other person in order to convince the other person that you trust them, and up the likelihood the other person will start to mirror you as well.

Proximity

Paying attention to how close the other person is holding him or herself is also a key indicator of how comfortable they are with you. When they lean in or position themselves closer to you, it implies closeness, comfort and interest. Conversely, when they keep their distance physically, it is often because they do not want to continue the interaction. They may be uncomfortable with you, or they may find that you are being dishonest or generally are unpleasant. If you notice the other person trying to take some distance, it is a pretty good cue that the other person is done with the conversation.

Eyes

Eyes are so incredibly expressive. Despite the fact that they have a relatively limited range of movements, you can tell the vast majority of how another person is feeling simply by looking through the eyes. Paying attention to where they turn, whether they dilate, and more can give you a ton of insight that you can use to your advantage.

Blinking

Pay attention to how much the other person is blinking when you are trying to notice their thoughts. The more frequently someone is blinking, the higher the likelihood that they are stressed or being dishonest, though rapid blinking can also occur when the other person is thinking hard about something. The people who do not blink, however, typically come across as being aggressive. Think of why you are told not to keep eye contact with large predators or animals when you confront them — it is considered rude, aggressive, and far too direct most of the time. The same rule applies in humans. If you make direct eye contact and do not blink, just holding the eye contact as long as you can, you are likely to come across as aggressive or dominant, and you will likely make the other person feel uncomfortable.

Eye contact

Eye contact is another of those unconscious cues that can tell a lot about another's state of mind. If the person is keeping gentle eye contact with you, meaning it is not a fixed, unblinking stare, they are probably interested in the conversation and interaction. If they seem to struggle to make eye contact or cannot maintain it, the other person would probably prefer the conversation end, or not happen at all. This could be due to being dishonest, nervousness, discomfort, disinterest, or just overall submissiveness. Hard eye contact that is maintained unwaveringly on the other hand, conveys aggression and dominance, though it could be seen as confident as well.

Gaze direction

The next time you are interacting with someone, pay attention to the direction of their gaze. The direction someone is looking tells a lot about where their mind is. Often, people look at whatever it is they are wanting in that moment. If they want that cake sitting on the counter behind where you are standing, chances are, their eyes will keep drifting to it. The same applies if they want to leave — they are likely to turn their gaze to an exit repeatedly.

You can also tell is someone is being dishonest or not — people tend to look to the left as they think when telling something that is truthful or honest, but their gaze drifts to the right when they are telling a story. When they look to the right, they are either telling fiction or lying to you.

Pupil dilation

Checking for pupil dilation can be tricky — it requires you to be quite close to the other person, but also depends on lighting and whether the person has lighter or darker eyes. When the conditions are just right, try looking to see what the pupils of whoever you are interacting with are doing. Since pupil dilation is entirely unconscious, it is a very reliable part of the body to read and interpret. When the pupils are dilated, someone is interested, engaged, or thinking about something. When they narrow, it implies distrust, disinterest, or threat.

Face

The face is incredibly expressive. Most people look at it in order to identify the feelings of others just because it is so easy to see what someone is feeling by looking at their face. It can tell you whether the person is lying to you or uncomfortable, or if they are at ease around you. Paying close attention to the face is always a good idea when communicating with others.

Eyebrows

Eyebrows should be studied alongside other body language as well, but just a quick glance toward the eyebrows can be incredibly telling. Of course, many of these positions are also ambiguous and can have more than one meaning, so look at the general body's language as well. Eyebrows can take several positions:

- **Furrowed: Furrowing brows is drawing them inward, creating wrinkles in the gap between brows. This typically implies confusion or sadness.**
- **Lowered: When you drop your brows down closer to your eyes, you imply anger, dominance, or aggression, especially when paired with direct eye contact.**
- **Inner tips raised: This is a major identifier of sadness.**
- **Both brows raised: Typically, this implies fear, shock, surprise, or happiness. It can also convey submission or attraction.**
- **One brow raised: With one brow raised, it can mean cynicism or contempt.**
- **Middle arch of brow raised: This can convey either relief or anxiety — pay attention to other cues for a more specific read.**

Lips and mouth

Lips can also take several different positions, some of which can mean more than one thing. Take the lips' position along with other cues to determine the specifics.

- **Slightly parted:** This is typically seen when the person is attracted to the other, or when the person wants to take a turn to speak.
- **Puckered:** Typically this can convey uncertainty or indecision.
- **Tight or pursed:** Typically, this indicates some sort of tenseness. This is usually a reliable sign of anger or stress of some sort.
- **Loose or relaxed:** This is usually more positive and has connotations of calmness.
- **Pulled back:** When teeth are bared, it is usually either a smile or a sort of snarl that is meant to show aggression.
- **Upward twitch:** Often barely even noticeable, this can show lying, disbelief, or guilt.
- **Biting lip:** This often shows anxiety, stress, or lying.
- **Touching mouth:** This is often unconscious and telling of a lie — usually the individual touches his mouth in an attempt to stop lies from coming. It can also be an attempt to self-soothe during a period of anxiety.

Hands

Hands have a myriad of ways they can be used, and because of this, there are several different ways they can be used to indicate what the person is thinking. Here are some of the most common expressions with hands:

Behind the back

This is usually a confidence pose. The torso and chest are exposed, almost as if the individual is daring anyone else to try to hurt him. He may also be doing so in order to be seen as trustworthy and credible due to being physically open — it conveys there is nothing to hide.

Clasped

This shows some sort of unhappiness or discomfort — typically uncomfortable or afraid. With clasped hands, the other person is often trying to soothe somehow. When fingers are woven together along with being clasped, the individual fears that there will be a bad result or news and is trying to brace himself.

Clenched

This is seen with stubbornness or firmness — the other person refuses to give in. This is also somewhat aggressive and can show anxiety and discomfort.

In pockets

When your hands are in your pockets, they are hidden. This is often seen as discomfort or reluctance, or sometimes a level of mistrust in the other person.

On heart

This is seen as an attempt to be honest. The speaker is showing that she is speaking from the heart. This is also easily mimicked, however, so keep other body language in mind.

Palms down

When palms are faced downward, it is often a confident, authoritative pose. You may see a politician stand like this while talking, with his hand up, but palm down. He may even add sort of chopping motions to punctuate his words as he speaks.

Palms up

When palms are raised upward, they are often regarded positively, especially if at the end of outstretched arms. It shows trustworthiness and openness.

Pointing

This is almost always an attempt to be authoritative. It can be turned aggressive with forceful jabs.

Resting on hips

Despite the fact that hands on hips is often seen as aggressive or unfriendly, it is actually the pose of readiness and occasionally authority.

Steepling

Think of how you would expect to see the big bad guy sitting at his desk on a cartoon — his hands are held with palms parallel, his fingers each resting against the finger on the opposite hand. It almost looks like praying, but the palms do not touch, only the pads of the fingers. This is known as steepling. It is a dominant position, showing that he is powerful and comfortable in his role.

Temperature of hand

When the hands are warm, the person is usually more relaxed. He has more blood flow to all parts of his body because he is not feeling stress at all. When the hands are colder, however, it implies that the person is tense or stressed and is awfully close to fight-or-flight mode. This is because when feeling afraid or anxious, the body redirects the blood inward, away from extremities. Of course, it could also just be because the room is hot or cold.

Touching

Often, we touch each other to convey closeness or familiarity. The types of touch can be specified even more — touching with the entire hand, with contact with the fingertips and the palm on the other person, the toucher is conveying that he is quite fond of the other person and relaxed enough for extended contact. Conversely, less physical contact, such as using only the fingertips, implies a lack of familiarity or comfort.

Head

It is no surprise that the head can betray thoughts — thoughts literally happen within it. You can see how much interest a person has in a situation bases on the position of the head. This is quite useful in group setting in particular, as people tend to direct their heads to the most influential people.

Chin orientation

The chin can be moved to show a wide range of nonverbal communication. When tilted up, it shows arrogance, or that the person believes he is stronger or more powerful. He is flashing his neck, the most vulnerable part of his body, and he would not do this if he were not confident he could protect it. When tucked in, the person is cueing that he or she is feeling uncertain and does not trust the current situation.

Nodding

When you nod, you are telling the other person that you are listening. It is supposed to show that you have heard what was said, but you are not yet ready to speak back in return. When it is done slowly, it implies that the person is patient and interested, happy to continue listening to whatever you have to say. The nodding may be sped up, on the other hand, if the listener is impatient or just wants to disengage. When the nod is just a slight dip of the head, it is usually used as a greeting to someone

Tilted

When you tilt your head, you often show interest in what is speaking. However, if you are tilting your head toward another person in the group that is not actively speaking, you are showing interest in that particular person. Often, this is done toward the leader of the group, or someone who naturally commands the group. It can tilt back to show distrust or suspicion, or it can tilt toward someone, showing trust.

Legs and Feet

When people are attempting to control their body language, they often forget about their legs and feet. Because they do not try to alter their legs' positions, they are reliable indicators. Take a look at some of these most telling positions for both the legs and feet.

Bouncing in place

Think about a child who literally bounces in anticipation of that ice cream they have been craving — adults do this too. Often, the behavior is muted somewhat, but adults will bounce in place, usually on their heels, when excited. However, the bouncing can also be restlessness or discomfort as the person tries to alleviate some of the excess nervous energy.

Oriented away from you

Look at people's feet and the way they point when you speak with them. If they are pointing away from you, the individual has lost interest or focus. They may also just want the conversation to wrap up. When this happens, try to identify what the feet are pointing at — if they point at the exit, the person probably wants to leave. If they point toward another person, they likely want to go speak with the other person instead.

Oriented toward you

When the feet are pointed at you, however, this means that the listener is actively engaged in the conversation. They are interested in what is being said and are happy to continue speaking. It can also show a level of trust in what is being said, and implies good rapport between the two of you.

Pointing toes/feet up

Sometimes, people roll onto their heels and let their toes point toward the sky. This is usually done in contentment, such as when on a phone and resting with one foot up. It can also show excitement or happiness as well, especially when paired with smiles.

Chapter 7 Brainwashing and Mind Games

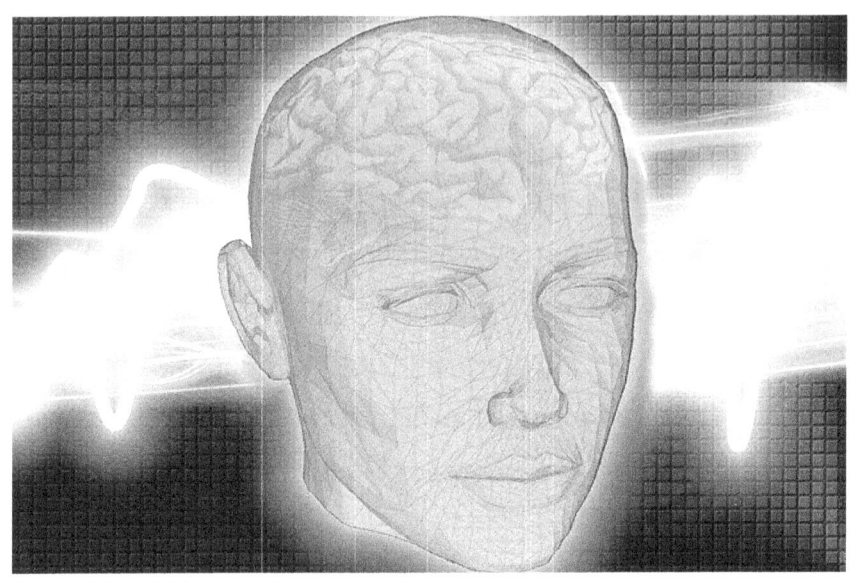

"Human beings have an inalienable right to invent themselves; when that right is pre-empted it is called brainwashing" - Germaine Greer

Brainwashing

In this guidebook, brainwashing is better discussed in psychological terms and how it is associated via social influences. Talking about social influences, it is the collective approaches used for influencing or changing other people's beliefs, attitudes and behavior toward something. Be that as it may, brainwashing could actually be characterized as a social issue in a severe form since it functions at changing the perspective of a subject without the subject agreeing to it.

To carry out a successful brainwashing, the subject has to be totally isolated and dependent since it has an invasive effect on the subject. This explains why most cases of brainwashing happen in prison camps or totalistic cults. The agent or brainwasher needs to gain complete control of the subject. He or she must be in absolute command of their subject's sleeping patterns and eating habits whilst satisfying the other vital needs of the subject, and none of these happen without the knowledge of the brainwasher. While the procedure takes place, the agent seeks for ways to break down the subject's entire identity, so it doesn't work right anymore. From the moment that identity is broken, the brainwasher strives to exchange it with the desired attitudes, beliefs and behaviors.

The idea of brainwashing is not generally agreed upon by everybody. If it works or not isn't certain yet, as many people have different opinions about it. Some psychologists believe that if the right conditions are in place, brainwashing a subject is possible. However, the entire task is never as severe as portrayed in the media. Several definitions of brainwashing exist which makes it really tough to know the consequences of brainwashing on a victim. Most definitions require the presence of some form of threat to the physical body of the victim for it to be called brainwashing. In line with this definition, most practices carried out by extremist cults would not be regarded as real brainwashing since physical abuse was absent.

The remaining definitions of brainwashing make use of control and coercion with no physical force, while aiming at getting the subject to change his/her beliefs. Whichever definition it is, pundits agree that even with all the conditions in place, the results of brainwashing lasts for just a brief moment. Experts also agree that the former identity of the victim is never erased totally with the experience; instead, it is sent into hiding and re-surfaces when the new identity is no longer forced upon the victim again.

Robert Jay Lifton presented fascinating opinions on brainwashing in the 1950s after observing prisoners of the Korean and Chinese War camps. During his studies, he concluded that his subjects (prisoners) went through several stages in brainwashing. These stages start with an attack on the victim's self-concept and conclude with a supposed change in beliefs of the prisoner. Lifton defined 10 steps for the brainwashing process in the prisoners he studied. These steps are:

Attack the subject's identity;

Force guilt on the subject;

Force self-betrayal on the subject;

Reach a breaking point;

Offer the subject leniency if they change;

Compulsory confession;

Point all the guilt in the intended direction;

Liberate the subject from supposed guilt;

Move into harmony;

A last confession before a rebirth.

These steps must be carried out in a completely isolated area. What this means is that all the regular social references the victim is used to coming in contact with are not available. Furthermore, mind clouding schemes like starvation and sleep deprivation will be utilized in order to speed up the procedure. Even though this may not be what's obtainable in all cases of brainwashing, there' is often the presence of some kind of bodily harm. This makes it difficult for the subject to think critically and independently like they usually do.

Different Techniques Of Brainwashing

As we now understand, brainwashing doesn't occur overnight but is usually a series of actions taken simultaneously over a period of time, which eventually results into a changed personality. Perception and behavior change, sometimes to such an extent that the victim becomes unrecognizable to their friends or peers.

The techniques used and the speed with which the personality changes depends on many things, but most of all on whether the target is being subjected to brainwashing against their will (in which case they'll naturally resist as much as they can) or whether they don't know they're being brainwashed (e.g. in cults) and believe all the ideas being impressed upon them are their own and that they themselves are making the decisions. This could be deemed successful brainwashing, as the victim is unaware of what's occurring.

Most common overt and covert brainwashing techniques:

- **Repetition and nagging**

It's hard not to start believing something or at least begin doubting one's self if someone is constantly repeating the same thing over and over every day, for months or even years.

- **Solation**

It is easier to control someone if they have no access to sources of information which conflict with the brainwashing material. If the target talks to someone about the ideas being imposed upon them and other people understand what's happening, they may scupper the chances for a successful brainwash. This tactic is often witnessed in abusive relationships, where one partner doesn't want the other to communicate with friends or family incase their motives are uncovered.

- **Blind obedience**

This prevents the victim from thinking for themselves.

- **Responsibility**

One central brainwashing technique is to make someone feel responsible for their faults and the things that go wrong in their life. If they make mistakes, do something poorly, or if things don't go according to plan, making them feel responsible leaves them feeling negative emotions such as guilt and shame, which lowers their defenses and opens them up for manipulation.

- **Guilt and fear**

These are used extensively as part of an overall emotional manipulation plan. When a huge guilt complex is imposed, we start believing we're deserving of any resulting punishment.

Self-brainwashing techniques:

Identify a negative thought pattern

Identify a negative thought or belief that's been holding you back. How long have you felt this way? Can you connect the programming to any early life experiences? Are you aware of how this belief has affected your life? What do you think your life would have been like if it weren't for this negative thought pattern? Do you believe you are what others tell you? What skills or abilities do you wish you had?

Acknowledging the damage

Be aware of any negative emotional, mental or physical harm this thought pattern has done to you, then make the decision to do something about it. Negative programming can be reversed, but it takes time, so be prepared to work on this issue for a long time if need be.

The Power of Suggestion

Much of our negative thinking comes from suggestions we take in from others. Think of how many times someone has spoken to you negatively, said you were fat, stupid or unintelligent? Eventually, when these suggestions are heard repeatedly they tend to became our reality.

We can reverse such damage by purposefully taking our suggestions onto a more positive path by consciously choosing positive beliefs. Whatever flaws you believe you have, they can often be reversed. One such way is to constantly tell yourself what you'd like to become, by verbally affirming (or thinking) how successful, healthy or confident you are. Eventually, with commitment, these suggestions can come true as our actions and behaviors gradually begin to follow the constant positive reinforcement we're feeding ourselves.

Repetition

Repetition is successfully used in self-brainwashing. Consistently reinforce positive thoughts about yourself or your self-image by repeating confidence-boosting words and affirmations throughout the day. If it helps, use sticky notes on your desk, inside your car, on the fridge, and other places where you'll often see them. Or, try chanting short phrases such as, 'I am smart', 'I am successful', 'People like me' or whatever you're trying to change.

Mind Games

When a person plays "mind games" on us, it is attributed to being innocent. Many people have come across this at some point in their life. Take an example when someone is planning a surprise party and doesn't want the other person to know and he does this by playing mind tricks in order not to give away what the surprise actually is. This is merely considered innocent and silly. Dark psychology mind games are not in any way innocent. Mind games in dark psychology are attributed to the hypnotist toying with the will power and sanity of his victim. This differs from other dark psychological manipulation in the sense that the manipulator is playing with his victim for his own pleasure and enjoyment and is not invested in what the outcome will be. His interest in the victim would be to test the victim so to speak. Mind games are used by a hypnotist when other forms of suggestions to the victim are not effective and may decide to use mind games which are rather less obvious to the audience. The manipulator may decide to use mind games to his own pleasure and amusement. Mind games are very effective in reducing the assuredness and psychological strength of the victim. The victim is eluded into thinking that he still has control. Manipulators are able to satisfy their twisted amusement when playing mind games. Such dark psychological manipulators do not see their victims as equal human beings and instead chooses to see the victim as a 'toy' and a person who can be manipulated and therefore, watch with amusement when victims do what they tell them to. Sometimes, a dark manipulator will have known mind games all his life and knows no other forms of dark psychology manipulation. These manipulators can be dangerous because they know not of any other option and therefore no need of changing and being more humane. Let us dive into the specific types of mind games used by dark manipulators.

Ultimatum

An ultimatum can be defined as a final proposition or condition. One, therefore, is presented with a severe choice. They are viewed more as demands other than a request. An example is, "Be more outgoing...or I will see other people". Certain factors will decide whether an ultimatum will be considered as a mind game. The three factors are one, the type of person giving the ultimatum, second the intention for giving the ultimatum and lastly the nature of the ultimatum.

Persons who give ultimatums and genuinely care about the persons and have a valid reason for doing so, and then it will fall under the non-dark manipulation. These persons will generally include spouses, parents, siblings or close relatives. However, if they fall into any of the categories mention it does not necessarily rid them of dark intentions from the ultimatum given.

What was the intention of the person giving the ultimatum? People with good intentions are often driven by the desire to help or assist in bettering the life of a person. Where a person gives an ultimatum to for example stop smoking or drinking too much, then this seen as good intentions. Being able to tell the intention of an ultimatum is difficult and so looking at the nature of the ultimatum itself is the surest way to be able to tell whether it is dark.

Dark manipulative ultimatums will involve the person doing something that goes against what they stand for and goes against what their self-interest. The victim ends up comprising their moral standards in the process. Manipulators test their victims to see how far they go in compromising what they believe in. As we have seen, non-dark ultimatums are usually to benefit another person and the does not have to go against what they know is wrong.

What is a dark psychological ultimatum? The person giving the ultimatum will be a friend, a boss or a person who the victim is in a toxic relationship with. It could also the form of a spouse, a parent or a sibling. The manipulator will often give ultimatums that go against the victim's moral conviction or that which can possibly be dangerous to the victim. Here, the dark manipulator will notice a disinclination towards something and take advantage of this to make their victim do their bidding. An example will be a girl who is not comfortable in wearing costumes or revealing clothes. Some of the ultimatums will be, "It's an only costume party, it is either you wear one or you are not invited". Some ultimatums lead to harm to others such as assault and even murder. At very extreme cases, the victim ends up taking his own life in completing a suicide pact in which the manipulator does not honour his end.

The External Break up

Everybody likes to be in a relationship where there is that sense of security and knowing that your partner is content. A manipulator will know this but will use these for their dark intentions. A manipulator will ensure that their partner will be powerless by instigating feelings of instability, and negativity within their relationship. This technique of 'The External Break up' is often deployed in a romantic relationship. It manifests itself when a partner continuously to scares the other that he or she will leave them. This is aimed at creating feelings of anxiety and instability within the relationship. This mind game takes the form of promised breakups, implied breakups and actual breakups that do not happen.

Implied breakups are those that are not expressly stating the words 'break up'. Instead, the manipulator throws hints there and then to create some doubt in the partner's mind. They can do this by making statements that exclude their partner from future plans together. Promised breakups happen where the dark manipulator scares their partner that they instead to break up with them somewhere in the near future. Words like, "Don't worry I won't have to deal with this anymore because I'll be leaving soon" show the intention of a breakup in the future. Promise breakups fall in between the implied breakups and the actual breakups. Where the dark manipulator mentions the idea of cutting ties with their partner, either by divorcing, separating or breaking up, but does not follow through then it calls under the promised breakup.

The actual break is the most severe compared to the implied and promised breakups. It happens when the manipulator decides to leave their victim without actually leaving in the end. They may pack up their clothes and belongings in the attempt to leave but once they see the sadness all over their victim's face, the decide otherwise.

After going through and understanding the tactic of the "external break up" we ask ourselves what therefore is the end game for manipulator when they use this tactic? The manipulator aims at having the upper hand in the relationship by creating feelings of uncertainty and lack of security from the life of the victim and therefore reducing their power in the hands of the manipulator. By repeatedly simulating a breakup with the victim, the manipulator is trying to test the waters of how far one will go in putting up with being treated like a toy.

In the end, when the manipulator gives in to the victims' begging for the relationship to continue, they make themselves look like the generous ones. This works so well for the manipulator because his or her victim is not thinking rationally to be able to figure out why they relationship should end. They are therefore willing to continues with the relationship. Many people do not understand this concept of dark psychology and why a person would want to continue to be in a relationship with a dark manipulator in the first place. The impact of this on the victim includes the likelihood of developing serious trust issues where they will have a hard time trusting another person. This could take a toll on the victim's professional relationships and family relationships as well. After a long period of constant threats, the victims become almost like a slave to the manipulator in which the manipulator eventually grows tired and moves on to their next prey.

Hard to get

And just like ultimatums, the hard to get tactic can easily pass off as being normal. Hard to get can be dark as it can be also harmless and normal. Hard to get when it is harmless it occurs when a person will want to make them seem trying to be with them is not as easy. They will do this by making themselves less available by not making to every date and leaving the phone to ring a couple of time before finally picking up. The 'hard to get' dark psychology is much riskier. The manipulator will use this tactic during the relationship rather than at the beginning of the relationship. Unlike the innocent hard to get where the intention is to eventually be in a happy relationship, dark psychology hard is far from taking into account the wellbeing of the victim. When used at the beginning of the relationship it is innocent because no expectations are infringed at this point. At this point, no one is dependent or reliant on either of the person, so no harm comes from playing hard to get. Further along in a relationship when things are going on well then suddenly a person is unreliable and often times tries to make themselves busy. This kind of behaviour is not normal because relationships are about making and spending time with each other as this will firm up the relationship. A manipulator will be very cunning and start pulling away when their partner us already reliant on them. The victim will therefore put an extra effort to reconnect with their partner. In the end, the manipulator has the upper hand and will use this power to his or her own purpose while the victim is left in deep confusion and instability.

Chapter 8 Neuro-Linguistic Programming

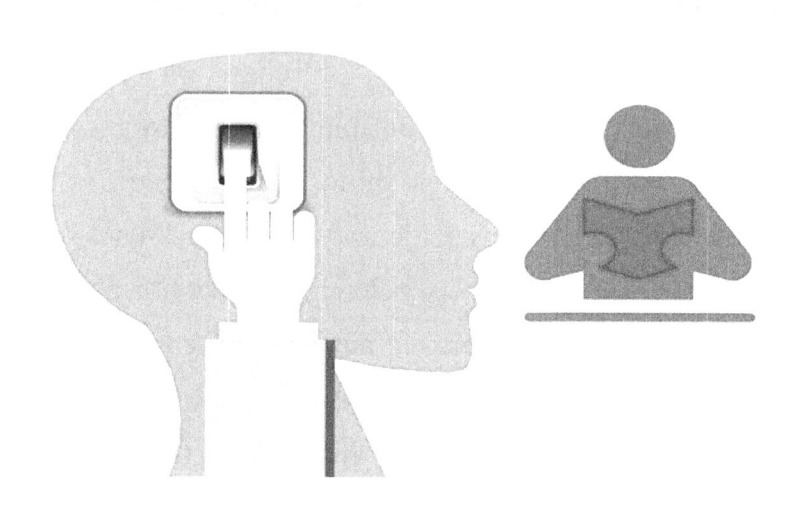

"It is the mark of an educated mind to be able to entertain a thought without accepting it" - Aristotle

This, like emotional intelligence, is a different sort of way to look at communicating. It was developed in the 1970s by Richard Bandler and John Grinder, and is all about exploring three major factors for behavior. This sees behavior as a result of neurological processes, language, and patterns of behavior learned over time through experience. These three come together to create neuro-linguistic programming, with neuro-

referring to the neurological processes, linguistic referring to language, and programming referring to the behavior learned.

It is believed that these three processes — thoughts, language, and behavior, can be tapped into and changed in ways that will strongly impact life. It draws influence from psychotherapy and is claimed to be able to treat a wide range of problems from phobias to learning disorders and everything in between. It can also be used widely in influencing others, making it a popular choice for influencing and persuading others to do as requested of them.

What is NLP?

In regards to persuasion, NLP refers to the ability to sway interactions with other people. It has several different stages when being used, beginning with establishing rapport and ending in getting the result desired. Ultimately, it is guided by non-verbal responses and reactions of the client, which can be used to first create rapport and later in swaying the other person to do what is necessary.

NLP starts with developing rapport, which is typically done through mirroring and matching behaviors. Remember when mirroring was discussed in body language? You can cue the other person to begin identifying more with you when you begin to use mirroring first. Following the other person's behaviors as a guide in how to interact with him or her, you are able to begin keying into their desire to like you. They are more likely to identify with and trust you if you are mirroring them. This opens them up to the next step.

You will then be gathering information about the other person's mental state. This is using a study of body language, or the way the other person may answer. When you understand the other person's mental state, you are able to begin understanding what their thought processes are, as well as the wording they use. This is where you begin to understand the linguistic and programming parts of NLP. You can understand the other person's mind through understanding their words. You can begin to understand the mindset based on wording, such as the focus on sensory-based metaphors, or focusing on certain tendencies. You understand their programming by watching their body language with their words.

From there, it is time to start cuing in on changing their minds. Remember how you begun the process with mirroring? Now is when you use it. When the other person readily mirrors your own interactions, you can begin speaking to the other person and mirroring the behaviors you want. If you want the other person to be more comfortable with, say, spiders, when you mention spiders, you make a subtle body language sign that you are comfortable. You may lean in a little bit toward the other person, conveying that you are comfortable as you mention the spider. The other person should mirror your own response, and as they do so, they are telling their minds that there is nothing to fear, nothing to worry about, and that everything is fine.

This sort of process can then be expanded upon to be used from everything from depression to creating self-confidence in another person. It is, essentially, swaying the other person to feel more comfortable with things that may have been uncomfortable before. It allows for you to sway opinions, behavior, goals, and more simply by tuning into their body language, ensuring that you share rapport, and using that rapport to slowly mold the other person's mind to mimic the one you are attempting to create.

Transformational NLP vs. Psychotherapy

Transformational NLP is a new combination that involves parts of NLP, various concepts of psychology, and spirituality. It allows for a combination of the three, mimicking the processes of psychotherapy while also allowing for NLP to be used with it. There are various parts drawn from quantum physics, psychology, and neuroscience, all of which come together in order to create a program that allows for the change of behaviors that are unwanted or negative.

Transformational NLP targets behaviors that are generally unbeneficial to you or that cause you stress. It works by recognizing that humans are a combination of neurological programming that keeps us alive, developed through millennia of evolutionary processes, as well as through decades of life experience. That programming can sort of hijack the ability to love and enjoy life, caught in a cycle of stress and pain that started long before we were born. Through transformational NLP, you are able to use NLP techniques in order to get past those periods of stress and those cycles of despair that were created with your ancestors in order to reach happiness and peace.

Transformational NLP revisits the programming within your brain and allows you to reach a point in which you are able to let go of your pain and suffering, freeing yourself from past pain and allowing your brain to move forward. It takes NLP techniques and methodologies and inserts it into a form of psychotherapy, in which the practitioner is asking questions and discovering what is happening in the patient's mind, and ultimately influencing the other person enough to lead to a change in behavior, beliefs, and a shift in identity.

Reprogramming Yourself

If you want to reprogram your own mind with NLP, the process involves five simple steps that you can walk through to do so. Each of these steps will help you alter your thinking, which will then influence your behaviors and moods.

Step 1

Stop and think about what has happened to you that you are trying to change. Think about a time that you were hurt in the past that is still on your mind today. Perhaps it was the end of a particularly messy relationship, or you felt abandoned after your parents divorced. Whatever it is, you should think back to it. For this example, we will say that you are hurt after your ex-spouse told you that she was cheating on you and has decided to leave.

How did this make you feel? Identify the feeling you felt during the last minute or so of learning that your ex-spouse had cheated. You may say that you are feeling hurt, betrayed, or angry. All of this is acceptable. Remember that feeling and that moment a little bit longer.

Step 2

Now, you are going to reimagine that last minute in which you found out you had been cheated on and broken up with. This time, though, you must imagine it as though it were happening to someone else. Watch the memory from a detached position in which you feel you had no real part. As you do this, imagine the following about the person that hurt you:

Imagine that the person is speaking to you and wearing a giant rainbow afro wig, is wearing underwear, and keeps slipping on banana peels. You want this stage to involve making the memory seem as ridiculous as possible. Now, reimagine the scene from beginning to end with the above in place.

You now think about your ex-spouse breaking up with you while wearing a rainbow afro wig and unable to stand up, as every time she does, she slips and falls comically onto the ground.

Step 3

You are going to repeat that memory to yourself again, though this time in slow motion. You want to really focus on the absurdity of the memory. Really see that afro wig and those underwear, and that the person keeps falling and is probably covered in banana goo by the end of it. Focus on all of the words being said through cries of surprise as she slips again and again on the banana peels.

Step 4

Now, you are going to think about yourself during this process. Imagine that you are able to watch your own reaction to the memory that has been overtaken by the ridiculous wig, bananas, and an absence of pants, and how absurd the entire process really is. Imagine your own reactions to all of these different stages — do you find it comical? Does it bother you? Are you still hurt and angry by it?

Step 5

Now, it is time to think about the incident again, without the absurd filter over it. Think about the memory that hurt you that you had been corrupting into something less painful. Does the memory still hurt? Or do you find that it is easier to tolerate now? If you were successful, you should feel amused at the entire situation. The feelings of entertainment that were related to the rainbow wig, the bananas, and underwear should return when you think about the incident rather than feeling any real distress.

Chapter 9 Applied Persuasion

"I think the power of persuasion would be the greatest superpower of all time" - Jenny Mollen

Now that you know all of the ins and outs of persuasion, it warrants restating again that persuasion can only be truly understood by putting its techniques and attributes to the test out in the real world. This, of course, is a book and not the real world, but it seems worthwhile to dedicate some space within this book to long-form, real-world scenarios in which one might use persuasion for one reason or another.

You may note that the language in the preceding paragraph is somewhat more measured than the language in many of the chapters that actually laid out the methods of persuasion. This is because this chapter will cover real-world scenarios in which inexperienced practitioners of persuasion for positive social change, on account of the fact that most people reading this will be relative newcomers to the world of persuasion.

This chapter differs because it is concerned more directly with driving home the point that persuasion must be **practiced,** and, as a result, it shows persuasion for what it often is, especially when you are just starting to practice it. In other words, it shows persuasion as inherently and fundamentally **messy.** As a result, several things will be true for this chapter that are not true for the majority of the rest of this book. Most significantly, it only portrays somewhat lower level methods or techniques of persuasion. As a result, there will be no elaboration on the practice of shaping cognition and perspective, though it, along with the optimization of the concepts, may get one or two peripheral references.

Two hypothetical applications of persuasion

Imagine, for this first hypothetical, that there is a person, a practitioner of persuasion, who has an employer that obstinately refuses to hear out the complaints, no matter how serious they are, of his or her employees. The practitioner of persuasion is not okay with this, nor is anyone else who works for this employer, as you might immediately guess, but no one knows what to do. This scenario is taking place in an American state in which very strong Right to Work Legislation has been passed, so they do not have any real recourse in legal, union activity, nor are any of them, save one who has not spoken up yet, particularly aware of the intricacies of political organizing anyway.

Besides these limitations, they are also terrified of being fired. As it turns out, their employer, apart from being a difficult and cruel human being, is also an adept manipulator, such that he is capable of stoking the normally occurring fears of termination in his employees to the point that they are meek and unwilling to speak up. One day, however, the practitioner of persuasion decides to do something after coming back from a lunch break to find that this employer has, on this particular day, decided to post a notice requiring, for no reason, everyone to note not only the total amount of minutes they spent on their breaks, but the seconds, too, **and** to add insult to insult, requiring them to pay, henceforth and effective immediately, out of their paychecks for each extra second spent out to lunch or on their breaks, of which they get less than the legally required minimum.

It is, very clearly, a terrible situation to be in, and many people in such a situation would quit immediately. As an aside, the turnover rate was terrible for just this reason, but the practitioner of persuasion in this story, the real focal point, actually quite likes all of his or her other co-workers and believes there is a method, through persuasion, by which he or she can ameliorate the situation for good.

His or her first decision is to attempt a sit down with the boss, but he or she sees immediately that this will not go well. The employer, absolutely beside his or herself with power, immediately senses a complaint coming and throws the practitioner of persuasion out of his or her office, threatening him or her with termination if he or she says anything negative to him or her at all.

This, very obviously, causes him or her, the practitioner of persuasion, to feel dejected and as if he or she has no recourse. Remember from the introduction that in all these scenarios, the practitioner of persuasion is a novice. In this case, this person had only in the past month read through this book, so he or she was not at all confident enough yet to contend with the problem of not being able to address his or her employer directly.

As a result, several months went by, and multiple co-workers quit their posts by virtue of the abuse they suffered at the hands of their employer. The practitioner of persuasion was about ready to quit, but, having spent these interim months studying and practicing in less stressful situations, he or she decided to give persuading his or her boss one more try. He or she noticed, the Friday after resolving to try once more to resolve the situation, that his or her boss would often come into work on casual Friday's wearing a baseball t-shirt. The t-shirt featured the logo of what the practitioner of persuasion surmised was his or her boss's favorite baseball team. Over the weekend following this revelation, he or she spent hours and hours reading up on the baseball team.

The following Friday, he or she mentioned offhandedly while he or she was in earshot of the boss that he or she was excited for some or another big game that was bound to come up soon. The employer, catching this, immediately approached him or her and began talking in earnest about the team. He or she humored him for that conversation, going into detail with his or her new knowledge of the team, while subtly complaining about a coach the team used to have who had been notoriously cruel to players, to which the employer emphatically agreed.

This was his or her first play, to highlight in his or her boss's mind the negativity with which he or she thought of those that abuse their positions of authority. The next time he or she came into work on a Friday, he or she began talking with the boss again. Somehow, despite everything, he or she was beginning to feel some compassion towards his or her boss, despite his flaws. With this compassion in toe, he or she began observing his or her boss and realized how pathetically friendless he or she seemed all the time. In their weekly conversations, he or she never mentioned going out with friends or really doing anything except watching baseball.

This is how he or she designed, from this, a plan of attack. He or she realized that he or she had to insinuate across a series of Friday conversations to his or her boss that there is a positive correlation to rage addiction and manipulation of underlings and being pathetically lonely and friendless. It was an easy sell, all told, and, because he or she only once directly pointed out to his or her boss that he or she was doing this kind of thing, and only towards the end of the plan, he or she was never yelled at, criticized, or fired. His or her boss improved markedly after these conversations and did away with most of his or her terrible and stifling office rules.

For the second of these two stories, imagine a friend group that has gone off the rails. To be more specific, imagine a group of friends in which, for some or another reason that has to do mainly with their collective inability to get passed or talk about issues from their past **as** a group of friends, each person has taken up drinking to an excessive degree at least three, sometimes four or five, nights a week.

To be clear, in this scenario, the drinking is not subjectively excessive. It is so bad that some of them are reaching the point where they could realistically die from alcohol poisoning. Several of them have already woken up having vomited in their sleep. Others cannot eat the day after they have binged alcohol; all of their binging is so extreme.

Now, imagine, in the thick of all of this, one of them realizes that he or she has a problem. What is more, he or she realizes that **everyone close to him or her** has a problem. Luckily for this group of friends, this person is also a somewhat studied practitioner of persuasion, which is to say that he or she read this book about six months back and has already utilized it in his or her life for good. Realizing that major interventions are needed and that no one will contend with the problem directly, on account of this group of friend's aforementioned inability to process or discuss the myriad amount of serious issues they all have, he or she resolves immediately to use persuasion on his or her friends.

Given the circumstance, try guessing what his or her first attempt is.

If you guessed that he or she attempted to use social pressure, you are wrong! Despite obvious signs that what was needed was an infusion of common sense into the group dynamic, he or she endeavored, instead, to try to individually change each and every member of this rather large and chaotic group of people's chaotic and dangerous habits, for which they all needed help immensely. As you might be able to imagine, this did not go over well. He or she labored for weeks and weeks to get three or four of his or her friends to sit down with him or her. Luckily, he or she was able, on account of his or her long term relationships with these people, quickly zero in on not only each one of his or her friends' particular psychic, which, here, is nothing paranormal and just the adjective version of the word psyche, weaknesses and limitations, but also all their main desires and the concepts most central to the chaotic parts of their lives.

That he or she got so far in such a relatively small amount of time is a testament to his or her prowess and natural aptitude in practicing techniques of persuasion, but, after having ascertained all this about these three or four people and having had conversations that were meant to begin the processes of change, he or she realized that nothing positive was happening. There was too much external motivation to continue drinking and dying for his or her subtle and indirect methods to take a major hold.

Afterwards, he or she realized what you may have already realized above, namely that he or she had been barking up the wrong tree, so to speak, and that what his or her group of close friends needed was some social pressure in the right direction to counteract and remove those negative external pressures to destroy each other and themselves.

He or she endeavored to take one of his or her closest friends, obviously also a member of this group of friends, out to the park on a Saturday, which was customarily a drinking day. Because this friend was somewhat more levelheaded than the rest, he or she felt confident inviting him or her out under more or less accurate pretenses, which were that he or she needed a change of pace. When the two of them went to the park, he or she mentioned offhandedly that this was a nice change again, in the context of a normal conversation.

How this snowballed is unclear, but in due time several of the key members of this group of friends started echoing the desire for a change in lifestyle, which arose in the group as if from nothing, despite the fact that he or she had spent the days following the pleasant trip to the park telling people in the group he or she had had such a pleasant time in the sun, while meanwhile his or her close and good friend, by virtue of his or her own personality, said to anyone that would listen how great it was to spend a day lucid at the park.

The limitations of persuasion

In slightly more time, the whole friend group started echoing the desire for change, and from this desire, an actual change came. It is worthwhile not to have rose-colored glasses regarding this case, which is to say that some people did not stop drinking to excess and that some of these people died of alcohol poisoning, but it was a measured success and in his or her own way he or she saved lives with the power of persuasion.

Chapter 10   Persuading and Influencing People Using Manipulation

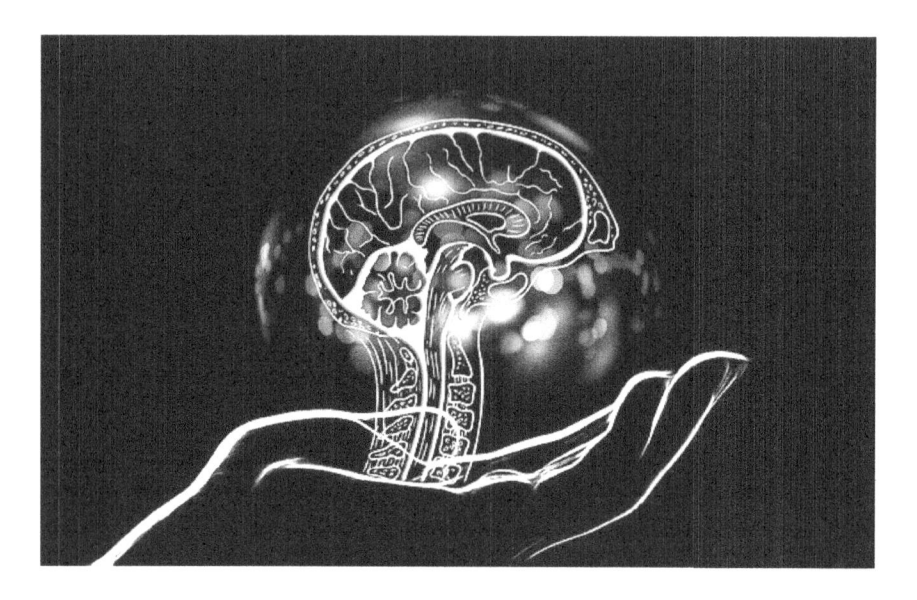

"The key to victory lies more in manipulation and cooperation than in exceptional personal skills"
- Yuval Noah Harari

Human being as a social being is in constant communication for many reasons, giving information, getting information, asking for help, making promises, telling your feelings and thoughts, or trying to learn someone else's feelings and thoughts, and so on. Communication is established within a certain structure and order. At this point, one should look at the definition of communication: Inter-human communication; It's the process of transferring information, emotions, thoughts, attitudes and beliefs and forms of behavior from one person to another through a relationship between the source and the recipient for change. As can be seen in daily life, in many situations where communication takes place, people either try to convince someone about the accuracy of the information they give, either to change their behavior or to convince them of something else because persuasion is an important and common reason for communication. The famous philosopher Aristotle defines communication as all the appropriate meanings of persuasion".

The concept of persuasion is defined in the dictionary as follows: Convincing, convincing; deceit; "Based on this definition, it will not be wrong to consider persuasion as a form of communication that is realized to achieve the desired aims." Indeed, when we look carefully, it can be seen that the difference between daily communication and persuasion is to achieve the desired goal. Not every communication phenomenon that is established in daily life is intended for persuasion, asking someone's memory only aims to learn about the person's condition and health. However, rather than persuading a person on a particular issue, it should be dealt with to uncover the desired change in the person who is exposed in the final analysis, which should be established with a certain systematic structure.

In the meantime, an important issue should be included here. It is also the effects of communication and how they occur. The effects of communication are:

1. Change in the recipient's level of knowledge
2. Changes in the attitude of the recipient
3. A change in the receiver's opens behavior.

In the second stage, the attitude change that came into the agenda is also realized in three ways:

1. Strengthening or strengthening the existing attitude
2. Change of existing attitude
3. New attitude formation

The effects of communication are often expected to occur sequentially and usually do. It is possible to see the effect of communication to a large extent in the change that may occur in open behavior. This is where the difference between daily communication and persuasion comes up. Persuasive communication is the expected and desired changes in attitude and open behavioral changes that will occur after the information is given. The attitude change that is expected to occur is determined by some attitude measurement techniques (Likert scale, etc.) developed in cases where open behavioral change can't be observed clearly or if it's not possible for different reasons, for example, an individual's Facebook, and so on. If it is desired to learn the attitude towards social media, a questionnaire consisting of expressions reflecting this attitude can be prepared. These statements; it allows people to share, enjoy the time, etc. can. It is possible to say that a Likert-type scale was used to measure the attitudes of the respondents to measure attitudes.

The concept and process of persuasion is a subject that has been studied intensively. In general, the biggest factors contributing to the success and failure of communication emerge as convincing communication and its proper structuring. With good understanding and knowledge of persuasive techniques; an educator, an advertiser, or a politician, in other words, it is possible to evaluate anyone whose purpose is to change the thoughts and actions of others. It should not be ignored that some essential variables exist in persuasion. Each of the variables in persuasion must be identifiable, distinguishable, and measurable. Scientists working in this field, these variables fall under two headings. These are called "dependent variables" and "independent variables. Arguments are made or occur with the communication process. We know what these variables will be, how they will be formed, and predict and produce their effects. Dependent variables, on the other hand, have to be done, and convincingly. We often hope to replace dependent variables with independent variables that we manage and control. Dependent and independent variables are called a convincing communication matrix.

The convincing communication matrix is a precise and complete data about all dependent and independent variables in human relationships throughout human life. Independent variables should be considered in many aspects and aspects of communication. However, dependent variables occur only when a person receives a persuasive message in terms of the information process. The main issue that needs to be emphasized about independent variables is the operation of the basic process of communication: "who, whom, what, through which channel and what kind of influences. The arguments that make up every convincing communication state appear in this case as "source, message, channel, receiver, and purpose. The dependent variables of the persuasive communication matrix are divided into six steps according to the characteristics of new behaviors, events, and phenomena in which the person is convinced. First, a convincing message must be presented. The second step is the participation of the target person in the communication, and this person needs to understand what is to be discussed. It's important that the recipient supports communication until the message is sent later and third. The fourth step is the understanding of the message, as well as the acceptance of the recipient or at least verbal adjustment. The fifth step is the most basic requirement. This step is the ability to accept until the effect can be measured. The sixth and last step or dependent variable is the ability of the target person to show the new behavior as open behavior. For example;

depending on the main objective of the persuasion campaign, the purchase of a certain product, the selection of the candidate or leaving a harmful habit, etc. they are always concrete indicators of this last dependent variable. An analysis in the context of dependent and independent variables can help organize ideas about persuasion. The persuasion process is analyzed at all levels of communication.

These steps are as follows: Source of communication, form, content, and organization of communication, characteristics of the channel to which the message will be delivered, ability and characteristics of the intended recipient and intended behavior and attitude changes. Thus, under these five headings of communication, the efficiency of the persuasive communication process performed under the six steps of the dependent variables of persuasion is defined and evaluated. Examination of the persuasion process shows the importance of understanding and attention in a way. For example; when asked what kind of connection can be made between an intelligent buyer and persuasion, he will probably tell you that only a much smarter individual can convince that person. In other words, the more knowledgeable and intelligent person can only direct the person's point of view to another party. This point shows the variables of the connection between intelligence and persuasive communication. However, other points that should not be forgotten are the role and importance of attention and acceptance in the persuasion process.

Persuasion Techniques

The basis of persuasion is to direct the other person to the thought you desire and to make it normal in the basic belief and vision system. To simplify, it is to make the other person think the way you want. That's exactly what it means to convince. If the other person thinks the way you want, you can take the action that you want to take, that is, buying a product or consuming a product. Located below are techniques to persuade and convince some of the most effective techniques effectively. Persuasion techniques are not limited to these, but they are important for efficiency. You may encounter many other techniques of persuasion, such as rewarding, punishing, creating a positive or negative perception.

1. Creating Needs

One of the best methods of persuasion is to create a need or to reassure an old need. This question of need is related to self-protection and compatibility with basic emotions such as love. This technique is one of the biggest trumps of marketers in particular. They try to sell their products or services using this technique. The kind of approaches that express the purchase of a product to make one feel safe or loving is part of the need-building technique.

2. Touching Social Needs

The basis of the technique of touching social needs are factors such as being popular, having the prestige, or having the same status as others. The advertisements on television are the ideal examples. People who buy the products in these advertisements think that they will be like the person in the advertisement or they will be as prestigious. The main reason why persuasion techniques such as touching social needs are effective is related to television advertising. Many people watch television for at least 1-2 hours a day and encounter these advertisements.

3. Use of Meaningful and Positive Words

Sometimes it is necessary to use magic words to be convincing. These magic words are meaningful and positive words. Advertisers know these positive and meaningful words intimately. It is very important for them to be able to use them. The words "New," "Renewed," "All Natural," "Most Effective" are the most appropriate examples of these magic words. Using these words, advertisers try to promote their products and thus make the advertisements more convincing for the liking of the products.

4. Use of Foot Technique

This technique is frequently used in the context of persuasion techniques. Processing way is quite simple. You make a person do something very small first because you think you can't refuse it. Once the other person has done so, you will try to get him to do more, provided that he is consistent within himself. First, you sell a product to a person at a very low price. Then you get him to buy a product at higher prices. In the first step, you attract him to yourself, so you convince him to buy it. In the second step, you convince yourself to buy products at a higher price. Their acceptance of a small thing will help you to fulfill the next big demand from you. After refusing the small request from the other party, you feel a duty to make a big request from the same person. This is usually the case in human relations. For example, you agree when your neighbor comes and asks you if you can keep an eye on the shop for a few hours. If your neighbor comes to ask you to look at the shop all day, you will feel responsible and probably accept it. This means that the technique of putting a foot on the door is successfully applied.

5. Use of Orientation from Big to Small

The tendency to ask from big to small is the exact opposite of the technique of putting a foot on the door. The salesperson makes an unrealistic request from the other person. Naturally, this demand doesn't correspond. However, the salesperson makes a request that is smaller than the same person. People feel responsible for such approaches, and they accept the offer. Since the request is small, by accepting it, people have the idea that they will help the salespeople and the technique of moving from big to small requests works.

6. Use of Reciprocity

Reciprocity is a term for mutual progress of a business. When a person does you a kindness, you feel the need to do him a favor. This is one example of reciprocity. For example, if someone bought you a gift on your birthday, you would try to pay back that gesture. This is more of a psychological approach because people don't forget the person who does something for them and tries to respond. For marketers, the situation is slightly different from human relations. Reciprocity takes place here in the form of a marketer offering you an interim extra discount" or "extra promotion... You are very close to buying the product introduced by the marketer you think offers a special offer.

7. Making Limits for Interviews

Setting a limit for negotiations is to provide an approach that will affect future copyrights. This is particularly effective when negotiating prices. For example, if you are trying to negotiate a price to sell a service, it might make more sense to start by opening the price from a higher number. Opening from a low number is not the right method because you have weakened your stretching share.

Even if the limitation for negotiations is not always useful, it's particularly useful in terms of price negotiation. Say the first number and get on with the bargaining advantage.

8. Limitation Technique

Restriction technique is one of the most powerful methods to influence human psychology. You can see this mostly in places selling products. For example, if a store has a discount on a particular product, it may limit it to 500 products. This limitation can be a true limitation or a part of the limitation technique. So you think that you will not find the product at that price again and you agree to buy that product at the specified price. The restriction technique is particularly useful in new products. As soon as a new product goes on sale, you can convince people to buy it for a limited time or by selling a limited quantity of products with extra promotions or discounts. People who think that the product will not be sold again at a similar price may choose to buy the product you have chosen thanks to the success of your persuasion technique. Persuasion techniques are not limited to these. Different techniques can provide more successful results in various fields. However, most of the techniques that we may encounter in our daily lives consist of the methods here. If you want to be a marketer, if you are trying to sell a product or service, you need to have detailed information about these techniques if you want to make them available.

Difference between Persuasion and Manipulation

There are many similarities between Persuasion and Manipulation as the two words confuse non-English individuals: Natives too. There are many comparisons between the two concepts, and because of the overlap, people think these two can be used interchangeably. There are convincing good people, and there are good manipulators. Both try to make sense and encourage others to accept their views. However, although there are similarities in manipulation to making a cousin or persuasive sibling, there are differences to be emphasized.

Persuasion

Persuasion is a behavior from someone else directed in a specific direction. You've managed to convince when you try to explain a certain way of behavior logically and correctly, and others accept your opinion that they think is of mutual benefit. If you have good marks on your test and you asked your mother for an expensive gift, you are trying to convince her to buy you a gift. This persuasion is convincing because it sees the logic behind your request and buys gifts. The salesperson is persuaded to sell a product or service to customers as he tries to create the need for the product or service in the customer's mind.

Manipulation

Manipulation is the act of exploiting the instability of others and misleading them to accept your point of view. Manipulation is not mutually beneficial, only advantageous for the manipulator. At the subconscious level, people strive to control each other in an organization or a family. Instead of persuading them for their benefit, they try to manipulate them. Manipulation can also be for the good of the person, even as a child's mother says that instead of eating all of them from the cookie jar, they can get a cookie. This creates the possibility of illusion, and your child can easily accept for fear of losing the jar without a single cookie. You manipulated the child's behavior for his good. Manipulation can also be bad, and manipulation is bad because the manipulator aims to trick and benefit from it.

The distinction between persuasion and manipulation

• Manipulation, managing others to benefit flawlessly.

• Persuading a particular person to change his or her thinking logically and rationally by reasoning with himself or by presenting arguments

• Manipulators can achieve short-term success, but people know who is manipulated and who convinces them in the long run.

• Persuasion is the art of achieving what you want by creating changes in the behavior of others, but it is manipulation. However, the difference is your intention.

• A person with good communication skills but malicious intent is dangerous because he can be a good manipulator.

Popular Persuasion techniques:

Brainwashing

Influence in various ways to alienate man from his thought and worldview, to think and act in another direction. Man is a creature that thinks and is very wrong at the same time. Because no living thing is as open to human influences, both from its internal structure and from outside, it is not as influenced by human influences. Brainwashing is the exploitation of the human being's ability to be exposed to internal and external influences.

Brainwashing can be classified as being performed in a long and short term. Short-term brainwashing: This is a method of brainwashing using medical and psychological procedures. The essence of this method is the excitement of human beings by preparing tired, sleepless, drugged situations in which the said things are accepted without details, uncontrolled, it is to constantly influence it and put it into behavior that does what is desired without discussion. The founder of this method is the Russian scholar Pavlov. Pavlov concentrated his work on conditional reflexes.

"Reflex" is the body's reaction to a natural warning. The spontaneous withdrawal of the hand's approach to fire is an example. Conditional reflexes are reflexes that are dependent on habit and gained over time. Pavlov used dogs as test subjects. Many times he gave the dogs meat just after a ringtone. In later experiments, it was observed that the dogs drooled with the ringing sound even though no meat was given. Pavlov has given dogs various conditional reflexes. In 1924 there was a major water disaster in Leningrad. Pavlov's dogs flooded the building. The dogs stayed for days at elevated water levels up to their noses. After rescuing, it was seen that dogs lost their conditional reflexes. It was this event that led Pavlov to the brainwashing method. He concluded that events such as extreme fear, excitement, and fatigue erased acquired conditional reflexes. The next experimental tools were people who were victims of the communist regime. Such methods were developed so that the mental angels of a human being were disrupted, their memories and imaginations were erased, and with the logic of making, a robot personality with other emotions was created. The first condition for this was to bring about the mental collapse of dogs in humans. This is a state that has long been seen in humans and is called mental collapse. Pavlov developed new methods for creating a mental collapse. Four conditions were needed to ensure this.

1. Fatigue: The first thing to do to brainwash is to tire. For this reason, one is prevented from sleeping during long circuits. For example, by keeping strong light on the face, both fatigue and sleep are provided.

2. Astonishment: When the mental activities are weakened and solved by the effect of this big fatigue, the poor person is rained for hours of questioning. His mind is so confused that the connection between truth and lies is completely lost.

3. Permanent pain: Wounds open on your body that will last for a long time. It is connected to the clamp or chain, and its movement is prevented.

4. Continuous fear: The ways to create feelings of tension or fear is resorted to. As a result of these applications, the exhaustion of the human reaches its limit and image dissolves. The out of control of the mind has the following consequences: Person is deprived of referral and effort. Memory clutter: Memories, interpretation, and reasoning skills; old habits are completely lost. The sequence of events has been forgotten. The nerves between the dream and the truth have become dark and blurry.

Melancholy: The mind wriggles in the grip of an unknown problem. One wants to commit suicide. Increased ability to be instilled: By taking advantage of this weak and defenseless state of man, they instill memory into a false form through suggestion. The new ideas they want to be believed are placed in the patient's tired mind as a form of suggestion.

The brainwashing process is now complete. Such a method of brainwashing has been used by the communist states, especially Russia and China. As a result of the brainwashing of the American soldiers who were captured by the Chinese in the Korean War; "We have seen the facts now. We were servants to the imperialists. The goal of communism is to achieve world peace. The Chinese couldn't apply brainwash to Turkish soldiers who were captured during the Korean War.

Psychologists have shown the strength of faith in the Turkish soldier, their unshakable discipline and commitment to each other.

Long-term brainwashing: This method is carried out by propaganda. Propaganda: Persuasion, persuasion, deception, arousing suspicion, and intellectual and spiritual oppression activity. It is a sensitive and special method which is applied by having a positive or negative influence on the ideas, opinions, thoughts, and feelings of individuals and society.

Propaganda means; satellites, sports, and art activities, the press, television, radio, and books, they are the communist countries that give the most important to the brainwashing of people with propaganda. Russia has allocated 1/4 of its national income to propaganda. The aim of the propaganda is the human's ideas, feelings, that is, the spiritual. The brainwashed men are the prisoners of the enemy with a stronger chain of captivity than the first and medieval slaves. A wicked man who has been brainwashed against his nation and state can't understand that he is the slave of the enemy until the end of his life because of the values to show that what he did was bad. The measurement of value is only determined by having national and spiritual feelings and owning them. The person who loses these values acts according to the desires of the enemy. This is a slave, or rather a robot. The robot follows orders, for a normal person, the order was given to him as, suggestion, faith, and decides through the filtering of national values and reason. The degeneration of the human brain instead of arms, deflating intelligence, and ensuring the nation's morale and spirit in the direction of dispersion will be directed.

Conclusion

Thank you for making it through to the end!

Within this book, you were guided through several different concepts. You learned all about emotions, empathy, and body language. Remember all of the body language you were taught — out of everything within this book, that may be one of the best skills to foster and develop. You learned of several different ways people can control, influence, and persuade other people to do what they want or need. You learned all about how people prefer to interact with others, as well as how to genuinely and naturally develop the sort of persuasion and influence that so many people desire. You were also taught how to develop several social skills that are of the utmost importance if you wish to be successful.

Ultimately, the information within this book should guide your own behaviors. Let this allow you to go through your life, informed and aware of how your own behaviors influence others. Watch the body language of those around you and see how easily they can be swayed by your own behaviors. Learn from the skills of negotiation in order to make sure that you are able to get what you want while still giving back to others. Remember how to keep your interactions with those around you ethical, even if you understand how to take over and manipulate them into obedience to do whatever it is you are seeking.

You can use the information you were provided for good. You can use it to better your relationships, your career, and your social life. If you understand how people interact with others, you can ensure that you are interacting positively. You can make every interaction with other people positive and fulfilling for everyone involved. Above all, you can develop the skills you need to naturally develop and earn your own sort of leadership skills. People will naturally seek to follow you if you develop your emotional intelligence. People will naturally seek to follow you and listen to you if you have advanced social skills. You can use all of that to your advantage to ensure that both you and those around you are happy with life. Use your enlightenment and knowledge for good, and go out there, armed with the knowledge you need to persuade others, both for your own benefit and for theirs.

Made in the USA
Columbia, SC
10 December 2020